BOAK & PARIS /
BOAK & RAAD

Entrance to 250 Cabrini Boulevard, Boak & Paris, 1936.

Boak & Paris /
Boak & Raad

New York Architects

Annice M. Alt

Library of Congress Control Number: 2014913131
ISBN: Hardcover   978-1-4990-5410-1
                   Softcover   978-1-4990-5452-1
                   eBook   978-1-4990-5409-5

Rev. date: 10/23/2014

To order additional copies of this book, contact:
Xlibris
1-888-795-4274
www.Xlibris.com
Orders@Xlibris.com
547332

CONTENTS

Appendices

PREFACE

In 1999, I signed up for a course offered at the Municipal Art Society on "How to Research a Building" by Anthony W. Robins, author, lecturer and tour leader about New York City. My husband and I had recently moved into an Art Deco building in Manhattan's Washington Heights. It was not only the stunning view of the Palisades and the George Washington Bridge that persuaded me to move uptown, it was also the felicitous layout of the apartment and the building's pleasing façade. I became curious about its architect, hence signing up for Tony's course. The first thing he taught us was how to find this out in the Department of Buildings records at the Municipal Archives. The name that popped up was Boak & Paris.

At home, I looked up "Boak & Paris" in the *AIA Guide to New York City* which cited the firm as the architects of the Metro Theater on Broadway at 100th Street, identified as a New York City Landmark. In Robert A. M. Stern's *New York 1930*, they are mentioned as the architects not only of the Metro, but of four apartment buildings. So I realized that they were not nobodies.

Now I had to go look at 3 East 66th Street, 50 East 78th Street, and 170 and 177 East 78th Street, their apartment buildings included in *New York 1930*. If it makes you a collector once you have three of something, I was now a collector of Boak & Paris, and, like many new collectors, I wanted more.

For weeks, I returned to the Municipal Archives to read microfilm of the Buildings Department logs of New Building Permits in Manhattan.[1] I also looked at reports of the Landmarks Preservation Commission regarding individual landmark and historic district designations and learned that the architect's names were Russell Boak and Hyman Paris. They had only one individual landmark, the Metro Theater; a number of their apartment buildings are within historic districts.

I wanted more, I wanted some sense of who these men were, I wanted a narrative. Fortuitously, I met C. Ford Peatross, founding director of the Center for Architecture, Design and Engineering at the Library of Congress, who suggested I ask the American Institute of Architects for a copy of their applications for membership in the AIA. I am grateful to Sarah Turner, archivist at the AIA, for digging up Boak's application. Apparently Paris was never a member of the AIA.

Boak applied in 1957, late enough that the application covered years of his professional life. Here I learned that Boak was born in 1896. After only one year of high school, he had been hired by Emery Roth, the very prolific architect of apartment buildings in New York. Starting as a junior draftsman in 1912, over the years he advanced to senior draftsman and designer. Boak stated that in 1923 he became an associate with Emery Roth with a 25 percent interest in the Roth firm until 1927.

I also learned from the AIA application that Boak & Paris, Inc. lasted from 1927 to 1942; from 1942 to 1944, Boak practiced as Russell M. Boak, and from 1942 to "present" [1957] as Boak & Raad, all in New York. Also Russell Boak and Thomas Raad became licensed in Pennsylvania in 1955.

---

[1]   I had completed my search for Boak & Paris buildings in the microfilm records before 2000 when Christopher Gray released his wonderful "Manhattan NB Database 1900-1986" on the website for his Office for Metropolitan History. Checking his database helped me identify one building I had missed. This database is an enormous boon to researchers, and I have relied on it to identify the architects of many other buildings.

This information gave me an architectural genealogy: Boak hadn't even finished high school, let alone college or architectural school when he started work, and it seemed clear his education was primarily from working with Emery Roth. At Columbia University's Avery Architectural and Fine Arts Library, Janet Parks, Curator of Drawings and Archives, showed me drawings in the Roth collection that had Boak's initials. Tramping around Manhattan, I could compare these buildings done for Roth to early Boak & Paris buildings and see the similarities and then, over time, the differences. Many of the first real estate owners to commission Boak & Paris had been clients of Emery Roth.

Andrew S. Dolkart, Director, Historic Preservation Program, Columbia University School of Architecture, Planning and Preservation, supplied many leads about the firm and its buildings. He also put me in touch with Christopher Gray who writes the "Streetscapes" column in *The New York Times*. In the summer of 2001, Gray wrote about Boak & Paris and my research. One of the people who saw this column was Gertrude Sklar Bell who had worked for Boak & Paris from the late 1930s until the start of World War II. Finally I could imagine the two men based on her vivid descriptions: Russell Boak looked like Gary Cooper, and Hyman Paris "didn't have an enemy in the world, and all his friends were tall chorus girls."

Using the digitized version of *The New York Times* available through ProQuest, I found articles from 1937-38 about the many buildings that Arlington C. Hall planned to build in the Bronx with Boak & Paris designs. I hurried the next Sunday to look at the cited addresses, and was disappointed: the buildings I saw appeared to be much later. At the Bronx Department of Buildings, I looked at dusty old ledger books, and found the New Building applications of the 1930s; there was also a loose page in the ledger with a list of most of these applications, and the dates on which the permits expired or were withdrawn.

For the Boak & Raad buildings, I read records at the Manhattan Buildings Department itself to locate those in Manhattan. The *Real Estate Record and Guide*, a journal published since the 19th century, was helpful for Boak & Paris and Boak & Raad buildings. The *Real Estate Forum*, a monthly published by the Real Estate Board of New York, was particularly useful for postwar buildings. I found leads in *The New York Times* for their buildings in Brooklyn and Queens, but have not tried to search Buildings Department records in those boroughs.

Some of my research hit dead ends: I searched in vain for any obituary for Russell Boak or his partners. There is probably no archive of the firm – Bruce Schlecter of Rose Associates, longtime client, told me Boak gave building owners his architectural drawings when he closed his office in 1972. And if Russell Boak wrote any account of his career beyond the information given in his AIA application, I have not found it.

Many people over many years gave me encouragement and very productive leads, especially Andrew Dolkart, Christopher Gray, Susan Tunick, and Phyllis Ross. Jean Arrington read a late draft of the manuscript. Others offered valuable suggestions: Andrew Alpern; Nancy Bruning; Joan Lince; Francis Morrone; Mary Neustadter; Matthew Postal; Janet Parks; and Kate Wood. I was fortunate to have help with illustrations from Jean Minskoff Grant and Judy Green regarding Minskoff buildings, and Bruce Schlecter of Rose Associates. Janice Carapellucci, my book designer, was very patient and helpful.

To talk to people who actually knew these architects was very rewarding. Gertrude Sklar Bell has to be mentioned first because we spent a day on her remembrances of Russell Boak and Hyman Paris. I was also pleased to learn about the mature Russell Boak from Daniel Rose and Elihu Rose, the second generation of the real estate firm of Rose Associates. I also heard about Boak in his later years from Charles Lako who was superintendent of the Westmore, an apartment building which Boak & Paris designed for Rose Associates, and where Boak and his wife lived until his death. The grandson of Emery Roth, Richard Roth, Jr. provided the insight that his father, Richard Roth, Sr. held Boak in high esteem.

I am grateful to all these many people who offered both information and encouragement. And especially I extend my gratitude to my late husband, Franz L. Alt, who never wavered in his support. The book is dedicated to his memory.

INTRODUCTION

The architectural firm Boak & Paris was so little known in 1981 that the landmarks designation report for the Upper East Side historic district erroneously listed William Francklyn Paris as Russell Boak's partner. This mistake was corrected in 1984 in the designation report on the West End Collegiate historic district, and Hyman Paris was rightly credited. In 2012, an enthusiastic real estate broker's ad reports that 152 East 94th Street was "designed by the famous architectural team of Boak & Paris in 1937." How had they become famous? Perhaps it is because when searching on the web for "Boak & Paris," it is likely that the first item that comes up is a 2001 Streetscapes column in *The New York Times* by Christopher Gray, entitled "2 Little-Known Architects of Distinctive Buildings."[2] From misidentified in 1981 to little-known in 2001 to famous in 2012! What is their story?

Russell Boak (1896-1981) went to work for Emery Roth (1871-1948) after only one year of high school. It appears that like Roth himself, Boak got his architectural training almost entirely on the job. Neither of them was a "white glove" architect whose first commission was from family; neither had studied at an architectural school like MIT, let alone the Ecole des Beaux Arts in Paris. But what an education it must have been, because while he was with Roth, the firm designed over 80 buildings, most of them apartment buildings in Manhattan. Boak started as a junior draftsman in 1912 and was promoted to senior

---

[2]   Christopher Gray, "2 Little-Known Architects of Distinctive Buildings: A novice researcher looks into the designs of Boak & Paris," *The New York Times*, July 15, 2001, Real Estate, p. 7. I am the researcher Gray writes about.

draftsman and then designer. The firm was especially prolific in 1923 to 1927, when Boak was an associate with a 25 percent interest in the Emery Roth firm. It is not known how Hyman Paris (1894-1966) was trained, but before he joined Roth he had worked for another successful apartment house architect, the Italian-born Gaetan (originally Gaetano) Ajello (1883-1983).

In the boom year 1927, these two young architects broke away from the Emery Roth firm. They took away from Roth a solid grounding in all aspects of apartment house design. Roth had perfected the layout of apartments centered around a foyer, instead of the old long hallway. Because Roth's patrons were building for the middle class, and only rarely for the wealthy, the apartment buildings had to be efficient. It is likely his proteges also learned how to please such clients, and indeed most of Boak & Paris early buildings were commissions from owners who had previously used the Roth firm.

As if to establish their independence, their first building, in White Plains, was in the Tudor style, not one Roth used. These young men were so sure of themselves that they were also the owner-builders as well as the architects of this building. Following that, they had commissions from many of the developers they would have known from their years with Roth. One other owner for whom they did much work in the 1930s had previously commissioned apartment houses from Gaetan Ajello.

After the crash of October 1929, some owners were able to move ahead with their building projects, with sometimes a little downscaling, if they had financing in place. Boak & Paris were busy until the nadir of the Depression in 1932. Gradually activity picked up again, and 1936 was an especially active year for Boak & Paris. However, the national economy had a downturn in 1937-38. This put the kibosh on some ambitious schemes for Riverdale, an affluent section of the Bronx in New York. Boak & Paris carried out two substantial renovation projects in those years and so survived the dearth of new building. They did some new buildings in 1939-40, but gradually work dried up as World War II loomed. The firm let its draftsmen go, and it dwindled to the point where Boak and Paris dissolved their partnership.

Boak formed a new partnership in 1944, with Thomas O. Raad, another New York architect who had come up the hard way, although instead of working for only one firm during his early years, he had worked for a variety of firms. With both of his partners, Boak was the lead designer especially of facades.

In 1944, before the conclusion of World War II, a new owner commissioned Boak & Raad to design a full block on the Upper East Side of Manhattan; this project was featured on the front page of the real estate section of *The New York Times*. Before it went forward, they did some single buildings commissioned by owners they had worked with before the war.

In addressing potential renters or buyers of apartments, real estate brokers use a shorthand in classifying buildings into "prewar" and "postwar." By prewar they often mean tall wedding-cake buildings, emphasizing the vertical, with so-called Art Deco ornamentation. Apartment layouts are relatively generous, whose rooms have distinct functions: dining rooms, living rooms, bedrooms. By postwar, they mean sleeker buildings, wider than they are tall with flat roofs, and combined rooms such as dining-living rooms. But this is only shorthand. Boak & Paris and Boak & Raad designed buildings typical of these two eras, but there is also continuity from the 1930s to the 1940s: some of the prewar buildings look postwar — flat roofs, and almost shorn of ornament. And on their early postwar buildings, there are sometimes prewar details like corner casement windows or in their place corner balconies.

Other things distinguish prewar from postwar for Boak and his partners. Prewar, all of the New Building applications they filed in Manhattan were actually built, while the entries for many other architects' NB applications have notations "Expired" or "Withdrawn." Postwar many of Boak & Raad designs were not built. Applications were filed and never built because the owners sold to others or changed architects. Prewar there was far more activity on the West Side of Manhattan, while postwar, the action moved decisively to the East Side. Postwar Boak & Raad had fewer commissions than Boak & Paris, but most of them were bigger and took longer to construct. Boak & Raad had some multi-building projects: the Doelger block of four related buildings, the Brevoort and Brevoort East, taking up a full block in Greenwich Village.

Postwar a number of developers shifted from residential building to commercial, and many of the architectural firms did the same. Boak & Raad tried to be players in this commercial arena, but their biggest commercial projects were not built.

Thomas Raad retired from the partnership in 1965. Russell Boak continued as Russell M. Boak & Associates until 1972.

*   *   *

A few comments on procedure. In general, the material is presented chronologically, with two exceptions. The Metro Theater holds a special place in their work, since it has been cited in a number of books about Art Deco architecture, and it is their only single New York City landmark. Also their commercial work was subsidiary to their residential work until late in their careers. It seemed best to treat these two topics in separate chapters.

Architects do not have a free hand in designing buildings; they must have patrons to buy the land and finance the construction. The story of this architectural practice is presented with information where available on the owners who commissioned the buildings; the story would be incomplete without them.

I have not used the term "Art Deco" in talking about Boak & Paris buildings. In fact, the buildings fit the category very well. However, the term was not used until the 1960s, and I was trying to understand how the architects saw their own style: I believe they deserve to be understood in their own terms. Gertrude Sklar Bell, the firm's secretary, said they simply called it modern, and modern, sometimes capitalized, was the term used in the contemporary newspapers and journals in describing their work. By Modern, did they mean anything more than up-to-date? Perhaps, perhaps not. Robert A. M. Stern called their work Modern Classical, and if we are to apply an after-the-fact term, this one seems appropriate: symmetry prevailed in their buildings, and they used decorative elements such as urns, Greek key and the wave pattern.

How shall we appraise Boak & Paris/Boak & Raad? While they were not the leading-edge innovators, they were quick to adopt new practices. They satisfied the builders who commissioned them; their buildings appealed to middle-market renters. They also enjoyed the respect of the architectural community. Their apartment houses add flavor and panache to the New York neighborhoods where they stand and most survive for us to enjoy today.

CHAPTER I

Architectural Genealogy of Russell Boak and Hyman Paris

At the height of the building boom of the 1920s, two young architects broke away from the very prolific firm of Emery Roth. Russell M. Boak and Hyman Paris contributed a number of apartment houses to the West Side, East Side and Greenwich Village of Manhattan. After the 1929 Crash and during the Depression, Boak & Paris designed buildings that actually got built at a time when the designs of many other architects were never realized. No doubt much of their success can be attributed to having clients who were able to arrange financing and so could give Boak & Paris much repeat business. What was their preparation for this career? Most of Boak's training was on the job with Emery Roth, while Paris got his start with Gaetan Ajello.

Russell Boak and his mentor Emery Roth have in common that both were trained in the apprenticeship system -- the norm in the United States until the late nineteenth century -- rather than in an American architectural school, still less at l'Ecole des Beaux Arts in Paris. Neither was a "white glove" architect whose well-to-do family could give him his first commission. It appears that Roth provided architectural training for his protégé Russell Boak in much the way he himself had been trained.

When his father died, Emery Roth (1871-1948) left a fairly comfortable life in Hungary at age thirteen to make his way in the United States. Unable to locate his uncle in Chicago, he got a job in an architect's office in Bloomington, Illinois. He then spent two formative years as a draftsman in the Chicago office of the architects Burnham & Root, working on the World's Columbian Exposition of 1893. Since all major buildings were to be in Greek and Roman classical styles,

> Roth was given access to an extensive library containing all the standard treatises on classical design, many rare publications on Greek and Roman architecture and many measured drawings of antiquities. Putting aside his desire to attend M.I.T., he stated, "certainly no technical or art school could have afforded me greater opportunities for advancement in design than the two years I spent on that job."[3]

One weekend Roth was alone in the office when the leading New York architect Richard Morris Hunt came in, needing drawings and a model of the Fair's Administration Building. Working late into the night, the young Roth prepared these, pleasing Hunt so much that he offered Roth a job in his New York office. This was a great boon for Roth: Hunt was the first American graduate of l'Ecole des Beaux Arts in Paris; among many commissions, Hunt had designed the first apartment house for affluent New Yorkers, the Stuyvesant on East 18th Street (1869; demolished). While Roth was in the Hunt office, Ogden Codman, Jr. was working on some interior designs for The Breakers, the Cornelius Vanderbilt mansion in Newport, Rhode Island, and "Roth was assigned to prepare architectural data that would facilitate Codman's work." Hunt died when Roth had been in that office for only about a year, and Roth then went to work for Codman.[4]

---

[3] Steven Ruttenbaum, *Mansions in the Clouds: The Skyscraper Palazzi of Emery Roth* (New York: Balsam Press, Inc., 1986), p. 23.

[4] *Mansions in the Clouds*, p. 34.

Roth's training with successively Burnham, Hunt and Codman gave him a grounding in classical and Beaux Arts architecture and practice in adapting historical precedents to the wishes of clients. When he started out on his own, he designed a few houses. In 1899, Roth designed his first apartment building, the Saxony at Broadway and 82nd Street. The seven-story building is "constructed of limestone and red brick with terra cotta trim in the Italian Renaissance revival style."[5]

The Saxony was followed by the Hotel Belleclaire at Broadway and 77th Street, for the same client.

> This building, which opened for business in January 1903, was even taller than the Saxony. It was supported by a skeleton frame, and at ten stories, was considered a skyscraper. It was a natural progression for Roth to become a designer of skyscrapers. Like the apartment house, high-rise buildings supported by steel or concrete frames were the wave of the future, and it was only a matter of time till skyscraper technology, as originally devised for office buildings, was adapted to residential structures.[6]

He designed several more apartment buildings in Morningside and Washington Heights. Starting in 1905, Roth developed a close affiliation with the brothers Leo and Alexander Bing, one of much give-and-take on issues of aesthetics and economical design. It had been standard practice for apartments to have long, narrow hallways; sometimes the entrance went past bedrooms before coming to the public living room and dining room. Sometimes the kitchen and dining room were at opposite ends of the apartment. Roth persuaded the Bings that it was preferable and more efficient to organize apartments around an entrance foyer giving direct access to the public rooms and maintaining privacy for the bedrooms. The Bings convinced Roth that placing windows in relation to interior rooms was more important than perfect symmetry on the facade. Roth

---

[5]   *Mansions in the Clouds*, p. 41.

[6]   *Mansions in the Clouds*, p. 44.

also convinced clients to enclose the water tanks and elevator bulkheads in masonry, an innovation derided as "Roth's towers."[7]

This was the growing architectural practice that Russell M. Boak joined as a fifteen-year-old in 1912.[8] Boak was born in the Bronx, New York, on September 25, 1896, the third of four sons of William and Eugenie Moreau Boak. His father was a clerk in the post office, but owned his own modest home, albeit with a mortgage. Russell graduated from eighth grade in 1911, and for one year, attended the brand new Stuyvesant High School. Designed by C. B. J. Snyder, the building had classrooms, laboratories, wood- and metal-working shops. Stuyvesant was a new kind of education, "the usual courses in English, history, mathematics, sciences, French, German and Latin [combined with] courses in carpentry, wood-turning and pattern-making, forging, and machine-shop practice."[9] Boak stayed only one year, and we do not know how much of this program he was involved in; school attendance was compulsory only to age fourteen in those days.

---

[7]   *Mansions in the Clouds*, pp. 47-51.

[8]   Biographical material is taken from Russell M. Boak Application for Corporate Membership in the American Institute of Architects, No. 12856, granted September 6, 1957; AIA Archives, Washington, DC.; and United States Census of 1900 and 1910.

[9]   *Stuyvesant High School: The First 100 Years*, (New York, 2005), p. 14. Lewis Mumford (1895-1990) provides a vivid picture of this remarkable school at that time: "In high school, there were a lot of young teachers who brought into the place the contemporary flavor of Cornell, Chicago, or Wisconsin, as well as nearer universities, people who were stirred up over their subjects and who would break into their routine demonstrations in physics with hints of exciting scientific news that would not for a decade or more penetrate the textbooks -- Einstein's first theory of relativity, or the electronic theory of matter, which made the old-fashioned doctrine of the indivisible atom look silly except as a convenience in writing chemical equations." Originally published in *The New Yorker*, December 4, 1937; reprinted in *Sidewalk Critic: Lewis Mumford's Writings on New York* (New York: Princeton Architectural Press, 1998), p. 44. Gilbert Rohde attended Stuyvesant High School in 1909-13; Phyllis Ross, *Gilbert Rohde: Modern Design for Modern Living* (New Haven and London: Yale University Press, 2009), pp. 9-12.

The idea of going to work in an architectural office may have occurred to Russell because his older brother Henry was already working for Bertram Grosvenor Goodhue, the noted architect of West Point, the state capitol of Nebraska, and many churches in New York and elsewhere.[10] Apparently Russell, unlike Henry, never finished high school. Boak said he attended Cooper Union (perhaps evenings) for one year, and did private study of architectural design and structural design for two years, as well as one year at the New York Structural Institute, apparently all while he was working for Roth. The application for membership in the American Institute of Architects asks about professional training (which could be "three full years in architectural work . . . in addition to graduation from an architectural school; or eight full years of such experience without formal education"), to which Boak responded:

> Employed by Emery Roth, architect, New York City, as junior draftsman in 1912 and remaining with him as senior draftsman and designer until 1923 at which time I became an associate with Emery Roth with a 25% interest in the business. I remained with Emery Roth until 1927 on this basis, and then went into professional practice as Boak & Paris, Inc.

In short, Russell Boak's architectural training consisted almost entirely of working for and with Emery Roth.

The Emery Roth archives on deposit at the Avery Library of Columbia University include drawings for 116 Roth buildings. His

---

[10]   Henry Boak (1890-1958) worked for Goodhue or the successor firm for a total of 25 years, as well as two years for Eliel Saarinen and then for Clarence Stein. Goodhue had become an architect by apprenticing with James Renwick, Jr., and Henry became an architect via his apprenticeship with Goodhue. Henry Boak held the positions of senior draftsman, spec writer and office manager. Information from Henry Boak's Application for Membership, American Institute of Architects, June 7, 1941.

obituary in *The New York Times*[11] estimated that he had designed more than 500 buildings, but his biographer writes that "the actual total was half that number."[12] Most of the drawings at Avery are unsigned, but a very few have initials. Nonetheless, there are enough drawings with the initials "RB" or "RMB" to get an impression of the buildings Russell Boak worked on while with Roth. His initials, "RB," appear with Roth's on the elevation drawings for 1000 Park Avenue of 1915-16, when Boak was still only a junior draftsman. For many years the most common silhouette for apartment buildings – this and other Roth buildings included – was rectangular, with pronounced base, shaft and capital, often reinforced by a cornice. The shaft would usually be subdivided by a stringcourse at the third or fourth floor, matched by another one or two stories below the cornice. Some of the windows at the lower stringcourse were often embellished, as here, by window surrounds of the same material as the base, and at the upper stringcourse by balustrades.

The two Gothic figures flanking the main entrance of 1000 Park, a medieval warrior and a builder "replete with masonic symbolism," are said to represent the clients, Leo and Alexander Bing.[13] Eventually, according to Tom Shachtman,

> Emery moved his offices next door to those of his principal client, Bing & Bing, and acted as in-house architect . . . Every year, Roth would design a building or two (or sometimes three) for Bing & Bing, now Leo's company, in every district from Greenwich Village to Washington Heights, from simple dwellings to palatial hotels and apartment buildings.[14]

The First World War curtailed building as material was needed for the war. Russell Boak told the census taker in 1930 that he was a veteran

---

[11] *The New York Times*, August 21, 1948.

[12] *Mansions in the Clouds*, p. 197.

[13] *Mansions in the Clouds*, pp. 47-50 and 58-63.

[14] Tom Shachtman, *Skyscraper Dreams: The Great Real Estate Dynasties of New York* (Boston: Little Brown and Company, 1991), pp. 101-02.

of World War I. For Emery Roth, the year 1918 was his low ebb, not only because of the war, but also because he had glaucoma operations and influenza that year.[15]

In 1919, the firm designed Temple B'nai Israel, at 610 West 149th Street, which was completed in 1923 (demolished).[16] The drawings for the exterior elevations do not have initials; presumably the design was done by Roth himself, as Roth's biographer Steven Ruttenbaum says it bears a strong resemblance to Richard Morris Hunt's Administration Building for the Chicago World's Fair on which Roth had worked.[17] The initials "RMB" appear on drawings for the main auditorium; mezzanine; balcony; main lobby; gym and swimming pool; detail of framing for copper cresting and turret of dome; and framing for marble railing in the lobby. The drawings for anterooms and roof have the initials "HP."

This was Hyman Paris (1890-1966), the eventual partner of Russell Boak, who "was registered in 1922 as an architect through The University of the State of New York, although he is known to have practiced as an architect as early as 1913."[18] According to Maria Brina, sister of Gaetan Ajello, "Paris started with Gaetan, begged him to give him a chance."[19] Ajello was born in Palermo, Sicily, in 1883, trained in Italy, and came to the United States in 1902.[20] In his architectural career from 1906 to 1924, Ajello designed over 30 apartment houses, all but

---

15   *Mansions in the Clouds*, pp. 62-63.

16   Roth Collection, Cluster 23. Temple B'nai Israel was demolished in 2005; *The New York Times*, February 13, 2005.

17   *Mansions in the Clouds*, p. 54.

18   Landmarks Preservation Commission Midtown Theater (now Metro Theater) Designation Report, [LP 1615], New York, City of New York, 1989, prepared by Lynn D. Marthey, edited by Jay Shockley, p. 3.

19   Interview by Christopher Gray of Maria Brina, sister of Gaetan Ajello, September 28, 1977.

20   Christopher Gray, "Remembering an Architect Who Shaped the West Side," Streetscapes, *The New York Times*, June 11, 2006, p. RE 7.

one on the West Side of Manhattan. His clients were the well-known developers the Paterno and Campagna families,[21] as well as B. Crystal & Son, T. J. McLaughlin's Sons, and – an owner who eventually became a major client of Boak & Paris - Arlington C. Hall.[22]

Ajello designed five apartment buildings for Hall in 1911 to 1913 and it is likely that Hyman Paris worked for Ajello during at least some of this time and so had the opportunity to meet Hall. The first of these buildings is at 420 Riverside Drive at 114th Street, 1911-12. Known as the Hamilton, its entrance displays "H" above the doorway. The three-story base is limestone, and the shaft is white brick with terra cotta window surrounds. This twelve-story building cost $1 million, the most expensive building of Hall's career. Gaetan Ajello often signed his buildings: here the cornerstone reads "G.AJELLO/ARCHITECT/1912."

Ajello used a similar palette of colors and materials in two other buildings for Hall in 1912-13, the Halsworth at 645 West End Avenue at 92nd Street, twelve stories, and its adjacent "little brother" building at 304 West 92nd Street, eight stories, both of which are embellished with many "H" cartouches on their facades.[23] The cornerstone inscription on 92nd Street is "GAETAN AJELLO/ARCHITECT." The entrance court for the Halsworth is distinguished by two large iron light fixtures from which large white globes are suspended. The apartments were from five to eight rooms; the five-room apartments had two baths, while the

---

[21]   Rosario Candela (1890-1953) also apprenticed with Ajello after graduating from Columbia School of Architecture in 1915, and became the main architect for the Paterno-Campagna clan. Andrew Alpern, *The New York Apartment Houses of Rosario Candela and James Carpenter* (New York: Acanthus Press, 2001), p. 23.

[22]   Arlington C. Hall (1876-1948), with his brother Harvey M. Hall, built many apartment houses in Manhattan and in the Riverdale section of the Bronx, starting in 1895. Obituary, *The New York Times*, December 5, 1948, p. 92.

[23]   Landmarks Preservation Commission Riverside Drive-West End Historic District Report, New York, City of New York, 1989, prepared by Miranda Dupuy and Margaret M. Pickart, pp. 104-06.

seven- and eight-room apartments had three, one for each chamber. All this luxury for a maximum annual rent of $2,100.

Hall also built two nine-story white brick buildings at 251 and 255 West 98th Street (1912-13), signed "GAETAN AJELLO/ARCHITECT." Even in these more modest apartment houses, each apartment had a maid's room. Especially the taller buildings have facades of refined elegance, but Ajello laid out the apartments with long halls, while Emery Roth at that time was already organizing the rooms around a central foyer.

Hall commissioned the only non-residential building that Ajello designed, the Claremont Theater at the southeast corner of Broadway and West 135th Street, to show photoplays, as movies were then called. The landmark designation report states that

> To acquire the site, in October 1913 the developers Arlington C. Hall & Harvey M. Hall promised to give the Hamilton (1911-12), an 85-unit apartment building at Riverside Drive and 114th Street, to Rebecca Mayer . . . In December 1913, Ajello filed plans with the Building Department for a theater, stores, and place of assembly. Construction began in May 1914 and was completed in November 1914. Designed in the neo-Renaissance style, it has a glazed terra cotta and white brick facade with round-arched windows, engaged pilasters, and low decorative relief. The entrance to the theater, located at the corner, features a pair of large cartouches flanked by eagles, as well as an elegant relief of a motion picture camera, draped with strings of garlands.[24]

The building entrance is at its chamfered corner, to catch traffic from both the avenue and the street. This is a device later used by Boak & Paris and Boak & Raad in their commercial buildings.

---

[24] Landmarks Preservation Commission Claremont Theater Building Designation Report [LP 2198], New York, City of New York, 2006, prepared by Matthew A. Postal, pp. 2-3.

While it is not known how long Paris stayed with Ajello, since his initials appear on some of the drawings for Roth's Temple B'nai Israel, he must have joined the Emery Roth firm sometime between 1919 and 1923.

There was enormous pent-up demand for housing after the end of World War I in 1918. In 1921, New York City enacted an ordinance to exempt new residential construction from real estate taxes for ten years, and building of apartment houses soared. Roth boasted that "During the boom years of 1920 to 1930 I was perhaps the busiest architect in New York City."[25] In this decade, the Roth office filed more than 100 New Building permits in Manhattan, mostly for apartment houses and apartment hotels, in Greenwich Village, the East and West Sides.[26]

Boak had increasingly greater responsibilities during this period, as senior draftsman and designer and then associate with a 25 percent stake in the firm starting in 1923. Roth's biographer explains how work was handled within the firm:

> At the peak of the boom, Roth employed as many as fifty technical men who specialized in the architectural, structural and mechanical branches that are required to complete working drawings. The office was so well organized, in fact, that each of those fifty employees became an expert in one of the multifarious facets of construction, and performed the same task over and over again as each set of drawings was prepared [such as stairs; kitchens; fireplace flues; etc.].
>
> During these peak years, the office was organized in a hierarchical manner. Roth determined the overall direction of each project with a preliminary layout and architectural

---

[25]   *Emery Roth: Autobiographical Notes*, unpublished manuscript on deposit in Avery Architectural and Fine Arts Library of Columbia University, p. 309. See also *Mansions in the Clouds*, pp. 66-67.

[26]   Office for Metropolitan History, "Manhattan NB Database 1900-1986," *http:// www.MetroHistory.com*, accessed April 30, 2005.

scheme, and then he passed these down to his sons and chief staff designer who in turn gave particular assignments to the remaining employees.[27]

It seems likely that Russell Boak was that chief staff designer for Emery Roth from 1923 to 1927. His initials appear on elevation drawings for five Roth apartment buildings in 1923 to 1925, sometimes with Paris' initials on the interior plans.[28] The Whitby, at 325 West 45th Street, was constructed in 1923-24, with three wings of ten stories each, and a penthouse above the center wing. Another of these at 135 East 50th Street, is called the Randolph, which some suggest means that it was built for William Randolph Hearst. A nine-story midblock building at 114 East 90th Street was designed for William Baumgarten:

> Each floor originally was laid out into four apartments which ranged in size from five to seven rooms. The larger units had a foyer, full-size dining room, three baths and a maid's room. This was not built to be a glamorous building, but offered its middle-class tenants generously proportioned spaces just steps away from the elegance of Park Avenue.[29]

The Hotel Cardinal at 243 West End Avenue and 71st Street is a fifteen-story apartment hotel for Bing & Bing (1924-25).

---

[27] *Mansions in the Clouds*, pp. 159-61.

[28] Roth Collection, Clusters 27, 243 West End Ave.; 33, 333 West End Ave.; 89, 131-41 East 50th St.; 90, 325-339 West 45th St.; and 95, 114 East 90th St.

[29] *Mansions in the Clouds*, p. 90.

Hotel Cardinal, 243 West End Avenue, at West 71st Street.
Emery Roth, 1925; initials "RMB" on drawings of the facades.

It is the most decorated of the Roth buildings with facades signed "RMB." In the neo-Venetian Gothic style, on the first three floors, it has windows of three different designs, all framed in intricate polychrome terra cotta. Above the first and fourth floors, there are heads set in roundels. Stained glass windows light the lobby.

Of a similar size and design is the 15-story building at 333 West End Avenue at 76th Street.

333 West End Avenue, at West 76th Street, 1925.
Emery Roth; initials "RMB" on drawings of the facades.

Boak's initials are on the 1925 elevation plans for this building done for William J. Hanna[30] and Albert Frymier. However, here the enframement of the Venetian style windows is monochrome and of less expensive cast stone. The roundels have, not heads, but only geometric designs. The facades of 333 West End Avenue show what can be achieved with coarser materials.

In 1922, the Roth firm gained a major client, Sam Minskoff, a Russian immigrant plumber who had become an owner-builder.[31] The first commission from Minskoff was the Myron Arms at 221 West 82nd Street and the matching Jerome Palace at 228 West 83rd Street, which Minskoff named for his sons. These are rectangular 15-story buildings in the Italian Renaissance revival style, with stores on the Broadway fronts. He next commissioned Roth for another pair of buildings, on Amsterdam Avenue at 201 West 89th and 200 West 90th Streets in 1924-25, similar to the two Broadway buildings, but with polychrome terra cotta like the Hotel Cardinal; here the windows are not Venetian Gothic, but Italian Renaissance. Another rectangular apartment house on Broadway at 101st Street is mainly distinguished by the fact that Emery Roth built the penthouse as a home for his own family there. Minskoff also erected 1125 Fifth Avenue from Roth designs in 1925.

---

[30]   William J. Hanna was president of a construction company which built schools, hospitals and prisons. Obituary, *The New York Times*, August 3, 1946. Two of his four apartment buildings were by Roth, of which Boak is known to have designed the facade of one and perhaps the second at 175 West 76th Street. Hanna's later apartment buildings are both by Boak & Paris.

[31]   *Mansions in the Clouds*, p. 67. Samuel Minskoff (1894-1950) came from Russia as a youth and became a plumber. He built his first apartment house in 1908, and became a leading developer of apartment houses along Queens Boulevard, the Grand Concourse in the Bronx, and Fifth, Madison and Park Avenues in Manhattan, as well as commercial properties in White Plains. Obituary, *The New York Times*, December 27, 1950. He also built residential and business buildings in Philadelphia, Baltimore and Washington DC. *Real Estate Record and Guide*, December 1, 1945, p. 4.

The skyscraper form evolved from New York City's zoning laws of 1916. The elevator and the steel frame made it possible to erect taller and taller buildings, to the point that light and air could not reach the streets below. In 1916, New York City passed the country's first zoning law. It divided the city into commercial, residential and industrial districts, and limited the height and bulk of buildings, with formulas relating to the width of the streets. The effect on the skyline was not immediately apparent. However, drawings developed by Hugh Ferriss and Harvey Wiley Corbett illustrating the zoning envelope were published in 1922 in *The New York Times Magazine* and widely reprinted.[32] Compliance with the zoning law could be achieved with series of setbacks as the building ascended, and this silhouette became dominant as the skyscraper form. Much has been written about the development of the skyscraper as a result of the 1916 zoning law in New York.[33] Most of the iconic skyscrapers were office buildings. But the zoning law also affected the design of apartment buildings and especially apartment hotels.

Apartment buildings were considered residential, while apartment hotels were deemed commercial. The presumption was that the residents in apartment hotels were only transient, so these buildings were permitted to rise higher and occupy a larger percentage of the building lot than apartment houses. For example, the Roth firm designed the apartment hotel at 39 Fifth Avenue and 10th Street in 1922. This building was 14 stories, with setbacks and terraces on its upper stories. In 1924 Arthur Loomis Harmon used the skyscraper form, with setbacks and terraces, in the 34 stories of The Shelton Towers Hotel.

---

[32]   For the impact of these illustrations, see essay by Carol Willis in Hugh Ferriss, *The Metropolis of Tomorrow*, (New York: Ives Washburn, 1929); reprinted Princeton Architectural Press, 1986, pp. 156 ff.

[33]   See Hugh Ferriss, as above. Also Sheldon Cheney, *The New World Architecture* (New York: Tudor Publishing Company, 1930). Cervin Robinson and Rosemarie Haag Bletter, *Skyscraper Style: Art Deco New York* (New York: Oxford University Press, 1975).

Emery Roth's apartment hotel the Ritz Tower (1925-26), is even taller, soaring 41 stories at Park Avenue and 57th Street, and has been called "a Renaissance palace made of rubber."

> Upon its completion, the building became a symbol of a new way to live for wealthy New Yorkers. Abandoning their private mansions, they moved up in the world, literally, into a building that offered residences more than three times higher than anyone had ever lived in before. Skyscraper living came of age with the Ritz Tower, fitting perfectly, as it did, into the glittering Jazz Age culture that New York briefly enjoyed in the prosperous 1920s.[34]

The man who commissioned the Ritz Tower was Arthur Brisbane, the highly successful columnist for the newspapers of William Randolph Hearst. Brisbane's bank required Roth to engage an associate architect who was equally devoted to Renaissance models, Thomas Hastings, the partner of John M. Carrere in the design of the New York Public Library and the Henry Clay Frick mansion. Brisbane later sold the Ritz Tower to Hearst, who lived there with the actress Marion Davies.

The tower had a pragmatic origin. Emery Roth had

> found it unacceptable to leave water tanks on high iron stilts and elevator bulkheads clad in ugly sheet-metal boxes visible above the cornice of well-designed buildings . . . He convinced his clients to pay the additional expense for enclosures by installing rentable rooms, of doubtful legality, under the tanks.[35]

In his 1929 book, *The Metropolis of Tomorrow*, Ferriss said that

> The utilization of upper levels, especially in the case of apartment buildings, has been one of the interesting results

---

[34]   Chapter Six of *Mansions in the Clouds*, pp. 95 ff.

[35]   *Mansions in the Clouds*, p. 51.

of the set-back regulation. Not very long ago, the penthouse on the roof of the building contained only the elevator machinery, the tanks, and, occasionally, living quarters for the janitor. The effect of stepping back the building was to draw more attention to the uppermost floor; roof spaces began to be planned on a larger scale as servants' quarters; a few adventurous individuals began to lease some of these floors, throw two or three of the diminutive rooms together and produce apartments which rather surprised their friends. The advantages which were in fact inherent in such locations -- increased privacy, exposure, light and air, as well as use of an outdoor space -- were increasingly appreciated; architects began to plan them in advance for use as apartments and, in course of time, realtors appreciated the point -- that is to say, rents were steeply raised and, at the present moment, the erstwhile janitor's quarters have become the most expensive rentable space in the building.

The use of terraces, fortunately begun, will, without doubt, increase as time goes on . . . [36]

The Ritz Tower could be built to such great height just before it was recognized that the apartment hotel category was widely abused:

From the developers' point of view apartment hotels were attractive because they circumvented New York's Tenement House Law, which included strict requirements for the height of an apartment building in relation to the width of the street on which it was located. No such restrictions were placed on apartment hotels [classed as commercial structures] and thus a developer could erect a much taller building than would otherwise be allowed. In addition, the Tenement House Law regulated how much light and air were necessary for interior

---

[36] Ferriss, *The Metropolis of Tomorrow*; Four Stages, pp. 72-79; Lofty Terraces, p. 94. Ferriss' prediction was right: between 1929 and 1931, nine buildings went up on Central Park West sporting the towers that give this boulevard its distinctive silhouette.

rooms (often necessitating a different and more costly configuration of interior space) and required that apartment houses include at least one interior fire stair for each two families (which took up a large amount of interior space). Since these stairwells were not required in apartment hotels that did not have kitchens, developers found that apartment hotels allowed them to include a more "efficient" use of the space they provided.[37]

Because so many people cooked in their "serving pantries," this category of building was abolished with the Multiple Dwellings Law of 1929, but not before a significant number of such apartment hotels had been built, including a number by Emery Roth and then by the young firm Boak & Paris.

In 1926, Sam Minskoff commissioned Emery Roth to design an apartment hotel in the neo-Gothic style, the Hampton House, at 28 East 70th Street and Madison Avenue. It occupies a relatively small plot of 100 feet on 70th Street and 50 feet on Madison, rising straight up with the street wall. The report on the Upper East Side Historic District gives this description:

> Fifteen-story yellow brick apartment hotel; upper floors articulated by stone trim and terra-cotta ornamental detail. Stone-faced ground floor pierced by shop fronts, some enframed with fleur-de-lis cresting. Entrance in center of 70th Street facade is fronted by metal canopy and flanked by wall buttress with Gothic detail which rise through second floor and are surmounted by cables. Corbel table above third floor terminates the base. Next ten floors treated identically, then a series of set backs give an interesting skyline.[38]

---

[37] Landmarks Preservation Commission Ritz Tower Designation Report [LP 2118], New York, City of New York, 2002, prepared by Virginia Kurshan, p. 5.

[38] Landmarks Preservation Commission Upper East Side Historic District Designation Report [LP-1051], New York, City of New York, 1981, prepared by the Research Department, Marjorie Pearson, Director; vol. I, p. 473.

This silhouette of a tall building rising from a small base culminating in setbacks and terraces, almost a tower, is a form that recurs again and again in Boak & Paris apartment houses of the 1930s.

Another building for Minskoff in 1926-27, is an apartment building at 1190 Madison Avenue at 87th Street. It rests on a larger plot and is twelve stories, and is again in the rectangular style.

Despite the absence of initials on the drawings for Minskoff buildings on file at the Avery Library, Boak's prominence in the firm makes it likely that he participated in the design of at least some of these Minskoff buildings as well as other buildings that came out of the Roth office during this time. The last building Minskoff did with Emery Roth was the luxury apartment building at 480 Park Avenue and 55th Street, completed in 1929.

Emery Roth's firm was enormously busy, and the Ritz Tower was a literal highpoint in the life of the firm, yet Russell Boak and Hyman Paris "broke away" in 1927.[39] Why would they leave such a successful firm?

Russell Boak's relationship to Emery Roth may hold the key. Perhaps Boak believed he had earned a promotion from associate to partner. But Roth's sons Julian and Richard started working in the firm about this time; Boak may have foreseen that Roth would eventually make them his only partners. Even they had to work many years before Roth made them partners in 1935 (and then only on salary not a share of the profits).[40] In addition, Boak's strength was as a designer, which may have been too close to Roth's own strength for Roth to accept him as

---

[39]   "Broke away" is the description given by Philip Birnbaum (1907-96), who said that "Russell used to brag that I was his protégé" after Birnbaum was successful with white brick apartment houses in the 1960s. Interviews by Christopher Gray, 1982 and 1990.

[40]   *Mansions in the Clouds*, p. 165.

a partner.[41] Perhaps the overriding cause was the young men's desire to escape the standardization of the large firm, a desire to march to one's own drummer.

We do not know how Boak's 25 percent interest in Emery Roth's firm was resolved. Did Roth buy him out, or did Boak have to renounce it? In any case, when there was so much building going on in the 1920s, it must have seemed to Boak that 50 percent of a small firm would be better than 25 percent of a large one. One thing Boak and Paris were able to take away with them was the respect of some of the Roth clients - including Bing & Bing, Sam Minskoff and William Hanna - who were willing to commission the newly-independent firm of Boak & Paris.

---

[41]   Another young architect who left Emery Roth about the same time was the Austrian-born Sylvan Bien (1893-1959), who worked on the Hotel Beverly (1926-27), recently renovated and renamed the Benjamin. Roth's biography states: "Roth was assisted by associate architect, Sylvan Bien, who subsequently participated in the design of the Carlyle Hotel [Bien & Prince, 1929-30] on Madison Avenue. At this point in time, it is impossible to ascertain his exact role in the creation of the Beverly." *Mansions in the Clouds*, p. 217. Bien's son Robert, an architect who eventually practiced with his father, said that his father had designed the Beverly, which gets credited to Roth because at that time his father did not have an independent office. Phone conversation with the author, May 2, 2000.

CHAPTER 2

The Launching of Boak & Paris: The Boom and the Crash

The first building by the new firm of Boak & Paris was in the New York suburb of White Plains. Looking up hill on Main Street, one sees a tower on the building known as Broad Park Lodge at the corner of Main and Westchester Avenue.[42]

Broad Park Lodge, Main Street and Westchester Avenue, White Plains, NY, 1927-28. The first design of the fledgling firm, Boak & Paris. As Pariboke, they were also the owner-builders.

---

42 *The New York Times*, September 4, 1927, Real Estate, p. 1.

Rising above a six-story apartment building in the Tudor style, the tower sits within a terra cotta battlement, and has four gables with half-timbering. It is surmounted by a light, with a weathervane atop. Facing Main Street at the third floor level is a crowned shield with a coat of arms dated 1927. There is landscaping on the Westchester Avenue front of the building, and a deep landscaped courtyard faces Main Street.

The building is primarily of red brick, with half-timbering of gables at the roof line, stone quoins, and a terra cotta bandcourse supported at intervals by four projecting heads. Windows are multi-paned steel casements. The peaked roofs of the two entrances are of slate, with carved bargeboards. Stained glass lights the outer vestibule, while the inner lobby has a fireplace, wainscoting and a decorated ceiling.

Tudor was not one of Roth's styles, but it was widely associated with the suburbs. By the time Boak & Paris designed Broad Park Lodge in White Plains, "stockbroker Tudor" had been stylish for suburban homes for several decades. R. W. Sexton wrote in 1926 that city and suburban apartment houses had different requirements:

> The design of the exterior of the city apartment house is largely a problem in fenestration. The determining of the location of so many windows by their relation to the interior walls puts certain limitations on the problems which makes it doubly hard. An architect must realize, however, that he cannot sacrifice the appearance of the room, with which the tenant is so vitally concerned, for the exterior design, in which the tenant has little or no interest. For it is a fact that the design of the exterior never "sells" an apartment. The design must be simple in the extreme, inconspicuous, but dignified, in good taste, and, above all else, well built . . . The entrance door on the street floor is best made the center of attraction, as it logically is. An ornamental door surround is naturally permissible to emphasize the importance of the door . . .
>
> While the design of the exterior of the city apartment house is really of little importance in the eyes of the tenant,

the exterior design of the suburban prototype enters very strongly into its success. Contrary to that of the city apartment house, the exterior design of the suburban type is, perhaps, even more important than its interior. It must suggest, as far as possible, a private country house . . .

The entrance hall in the suburban apartment house is of much less importance than in the city house. It acts more as a passage or go-between. The impression that is formed in the hall of a private house, and also, of a city apartment house, is formed by the exterior design of the suburban apartment house.[43]

Contrary to Sexton's generalization, in this apartment house in White Plains Boak & Paris incorporated both the city and the suburban features -- the exterior is embellished with many Tudor details, and it also has impressive lobbies that could vie with some in Manhattan.

Who commissioned this distinctive Tudor apartment house? In April 1927, the Pariboke Realty Corp., of 1440 Broadway, New York City, submitted an application to erect an apartment house from plans drawn by Paris & Boak of 2952 Marion Ave., [the Bronx] New York City. White Plains rejected the application for being too close to Main Street. Pariboke Realty filed a new application in June 1927 with revised plans drawn by Boak & Paris, architects; both the owner-builder and the architects now had the same address, 11 West 42nd Street, in New York City, and Russell M. Boak signed as secretary of the Pariboke Realty

---

43   R. W. Sexton, *American Apartment Houses of Today* (New York, Architectural Book Publishing Co., Inc. 1926), pp. XIV, XXIII-XXV. City apartments mean primarily apartments in Manhattan, while suburban apartments include garden apartments in the outer boroughs of the Bronx and Queens, and the northern part of Manhattan, such as Hudson View Gardens (1924-25, George F. Pelham, architect).

Corp.[44] Since they were their own bosses on this first job, they could design it as a showcase to impress future clients. The fledgling firm of Boak & Paris put up their first independent design at an estimated cost of $550,000 plus the cost of land of about $151,000. While they probably had a mortgage for most of the construction costs, they must have been required to make at least a small down-payment. It is certainly possible that the settlement with Emery Roth when Russell Boak left the Roth firm was the source of that cash. In 1928 when Broad Park Lodge was for sale, land and building were appraised at $900,000.[45]

In August 1927, before the White Plains building was underway, Boak & Paris applied to build a 15-story apartment building in New York for Hanna and Frymier. The building at the northeast corner of West 106th Street and Broadway was projected to cost one and a half million dollars.[46]

---

[44]   City of White Plains, N.Y., Bureau of Buildings, Permit No. 5967. Construction would have started after September 1927 when an application to demolish a frame dwelling was filed, and was completed by October 13, 1928 when Certificate of Occupancy 1013 was issued.

[45]   Advertisement offering mortgage certificates at 5-1/2 percent by New York Title and Mortgage Company, *The New York Times*, November 1, 1928, p. 2.

[46]   Architects' commission for drawings and specifications plus construction supervision would have been 6 percent, or $90,000; if Hanna and Frymier did their own construction supervision, Boak & Paris' commission would have been 4-1/2 percent or $67,500. Percentages from New York Society of Architects Code of Professional Practice and Schedule of Reasonable Minimum Charges in General Practice, 1927 edition.

225 West 106th Street, at Broadway, 1927.

225 West 106th has much in common with the two 1925 buildings at 175 West 76th Street and 333 West End Avenue that the Roth firm had done for Hanna: they are all rectangular buildings in the Italian Renaissance style characteristic of Roth buildings of that time, with discrete base, shaft and capital, their essential horizontality emphasized by their prominent cornices.

As befits a 15-story apartment house with a bank on the ground floor, 225 West 106th is a very solid building. It has a two-story base of limestone, red brick facade on its shaft, with a stringcourse above the twelfth floor, and a cornice. Although it is built to the maximum permissible height of 150 feet, it is wider than high on both fronts and thereby is strongly horizontal. Balconies and window surrounds are of terra cotta, with men's heads (shall we say perhaps Florentine bankers?) between the third and fourth floors and pelican heads between the fourth and fifth floors. Another set of balconies appears at the twelfth floor level, and a terra cotta bandcourse separates the twelfth and thirteenth floors. The terra cotta is matte glaze in a color very close to the limestone.

Terra cotta at 13th through 16th floors of 225 West 106th Street.

There is a stained glass lunette above the entrance door to the apartment house. The lobby extends under two of the three wings of the building, with windows to a rear courtyard. The floors are terrazzo. Marble surrounds the elevator door. Wrought iron is used for railings, a chandelier and a pier table. Although the interior of the bank at the corner is no longer visible (the drugstore has installed dropped ceilings), it is clear from the building's lobby that Boak & Paris were responsible for its interior design details. Indeed, throughout their practice, lobbies and facades are well-coordinated designs.

At 106th Street, Broadway diagonals to the west so some bedrooms in the west wing of this building are angled,[47] just one of the many irregular plots challenging the skills of Boak & Paris. Another characteristic of Boak & Paris designs is present here -- a bathroom for every bedroom, which was not then commonly a feature of middle class apartments.

An eleven-story building at 139 East 94th Street and Lexington Avenue was built in 1927-28. Limestone covers a ground floor base, with storefronts on the avenue side. There is a bandcourse supported by pilasters from the third to the fourth floor. The shaft is red brick, with another bandcourse above the tenth floor, with a top floor and a penthouse. The owner was Lexington Estates, Inc. whose president was Samuel Levy, an owner who had commissioned Emery Roth to design a 14-story building at 93rd Street and Park Avenue in 1924 – here again an instance of Boak & Paris getting a commission from an old client of Emery Roth. When apartment 11B was featured in *The New York Times* as "On the Market" in 2012, it was noted as a fault that both bathrooms are en-suite, yet the price was $1.5 million.[48]

Boak & Paris designed a luxury building overlooking Brooklyn's Prospect Park West, in the Venetian style with which they were very familiar. Nine Prospect Park West, southwest corner of President Street, was built in 1928-29 and opened less than a month before the stock market crash in October 1929. An early announcement about the building was that there would be three suites per floor, of four to nine rooms.[49] Indeed floor plans on file at Columbia University's Avery

---

47   Michael Henry Adams writes of the Beaumont, also on an irregular plot, at 730 Riverside Drive, by George and Edward Blum, 1912, "great trouble was expended to avoid excessively long passages and oddly shaped rooms. When absolutely unavoidable, slight irregularities were permitted in large bedrooms and entryways. However, reception rooms are always strictly symmetrical . . . " *Harlem Lost and Found: An Architectural and Social History, 1765-1915* (New York: The Monacelli Press, 2002), p. 176.

48   *The New York Times*, April 8, 2012, Real Estate, p. 3

49   *The New York Times*, February 10, 1929, Real Estate, p. 2.

Library indicate that layout.[50] It was typical of Boak & Paris buildings that a mix of large and small apartments permitted families of different sizes and even incomes to live side by side. As built, on most of the 15 floors at Prospect Park West, there are only two apartments per floor, of nine rooms each with four or five bathrooms. Indicative of the wealth of the prospective renters is the fact that these apartments included two servants' rooms and servants' baths. There were three doctors' offices on the first floor.

Its fronts on the Park and President Street are highly decorated. The two-story base appears to be of limestone, with a red brick facade above. There are balconies with window surrounds at the fourth story, repeated again at the thirteenth story. Quoining extends from the top of the base to the cornice. The owner-builder was Samuel Wander, who "headed the building interests which last Fall completed a 15-story building two blocks away at 27 Prospect Park West."[51] The earlier building is credited to Emery Roth, but since it may have been designed before Boak and Paris left Roth, they might also have been involved in 27 Prospect Park West.

The Wall Street crash of October 29, 1929, signals the beginning of the Depression, which eventually stopped nearly all construction. However, if financing for projects had been arranged prior to the Crash, building could go forward. In anticipation of the opening of the Eighth Avenue subway, Bing & Bing had assembled 150,000 square feet in Greenwich Village.

> Located as it is, residents on or near Abingdon, Sheridan and Jackson Squares will travel counter to the major morning and evening traffic and, since they are very close to the large business centers, travel will be quick and comfortable . . . We intend to build a group of 16-story fireproof apartments and apartment hotels which will be not only the equal in every way of the better type of similar structures to be found in

---

[50]   New York Real Estate Brochure Collection, Avery Architectural and Fine Arts Library, Columbia University, 9 Prospect Park West.

[51]   *The New York Times*, February 10, 1929, Real Estate, p. 2.

the already-established sections of this city; but they will also incorporate a program of advanced features not as yet to be found anywhere . . . The development planned by Bing & Bing, it is reported, will involve an aggregate expenditure of $40,000,000.[52]

By November 1930, Bing & Bing had five of these Greenwich Village apartment houses underway, as well as other buildings on East 73rd and East 28th Streets, all then worth a total of over $10,000,000. The drop in value can be attributed to not developing some of the Village sites and redesign for more modest apartments; but it must also reflect the severe drop in the costs of both labor and material – money goes farther in a depression.

As built, the Greenwich Village buildings had apartments of one to four rooms, with a few five-room units. The Bings spread the commissions among several architects: Emery Roth (two buildings), Robert T. Lyons (one) and Boak & Paris (two).[53]

A New Yorker column about "New Apartments" reports of these five Bing & Bing buildings that

> . . . most of them [are] on corner sites and overlooking parks, which gives them more light and sunshine than is usual. They also have wide foyers, spacious living-rooms, and completely equipped kitchens. The closets are enormous, some as large as fifty square feet and are fitted with hat and shoe-racks and linen shelves. The hall closets are supplied with umbrella racks and guest mirrors, as well as trays for powder, combs, and brushes. The baths have cream-colored tiles halfway up, and the remaining space is covered with the most charming Thibaut wallpapers I have seen anywhere.[54]

---

[52]   *Real Estate Record and Guide*, April 6, 1929, p. 7.

[53]   Bing & Bing felt confidence in the demand for two- to four-room apartments. *The New York Times*, November 30, 1930, Real Estate, p. 1.

[54]   *The New Yorker*, August 29, 1931.

One of these, the apartment hotel at 302 West 12th Street at Eighth Avenue opposite Abingdon Square - an irregular site - has 16 stories and penthouse culminating in a tower.

302 West 12th Street, at Eighth Avenue, 1929-31.

It has the tripartite elements of the rectangular apartment house style: base, shaft and cornice, here surmounted by the stepped-back penthouse floor and central tower. "Two windows on each side set above a continuous stone bandcourse, at fourth floor level, have elaborate stone enframements of original design."[55] The window surrounds are echoed above at the fourteenth floor by balustrades. There are stores both on the avenue and the street. The entrance is recessed, with a revolving door flanked by side doors.

In several lines, the living room is entered from the foyer by walking down two steps, which became known as the sunken or dropped living room.[56] This alignment makes the living room seem bigger than it is, since the eye sees the combined length of the gallery and living room. Schwartz & Gross used this feature in their design of 55 Central Park West (1929-30): " . . . the original rental brochure . . . shows the dropped living room almost completely open to the entrance gallery -- a definite departure from traditional planning, in which the gallery was held as a completely distinct room."[57] Boak & Paris filed their plans for 302 West 12th Street earlier in 1929 than Schwartz & Gross filed for 55 Central Park West.

The second of these Bing & Bing commissions is 45 Christopher Street, another apartment hotel of 17 stories with setbacks and penthouses. The Greenwich Village Historic District report notes that

> . . . except for the doorway [it] has a symmetrical facade with a high, central tower rising above the top floor. The first floor consists of shops, and the main accent of the building is to be found in the vertical emphasis given to the four central windows, terminating in a pair of balconies at the fourteenth floor.[58]

---

[55]   Landmarks Preservation Commission Greenwich Village Historic District Designation Report [LP 0489], New York, City of New York, 1969, Area 8, page 338.

[56]   Here the sunken living room is not apparent from the street, as it was in later buildings where the living room windows are lower than those of other rooms.

[57]   Christopher Gray, "The Changing Colors of an Art Deco Landmark," Streetscapes, *The New York Times*, July 11, 1999. The original brochure is in the collection of Andrew Alpern, apartment house historian.

[58]   Landmark Preservation Commission Greenwich Village Historic District Designation Report [LP 0489], New York, City of New York, 1969, Area 4, p. 117.

Again some units in this building have a sunken living room open to the foyer.

Their 16-story building midblock between Columbus and Amsterdam Avenues at 127 West 96th Street is rectangular, with a cornice and a flat roof. Built in 1929-30 by Ralph Ciluzzi at a cost of $750,000, its red brick is articulated with terra cotta stringcourses at the third and thirteenth floors, with pelicans in the lower stringcourse. The lobby has Batchelder tiles.[59] The apartments are studio to two bedrooms.

The Multiple Dwellings Law of 1929 eliminated the differences between tenements (for the poor) and apartment buildings (for the more affluent) and abolished the category of apartment hotel. The uniform requirements for residences raised the permissible height for apartment buildings. In their next building for William Hanna, Boak & Paris took advantage of the new height limit of 178 feet to create the more vertical 444 Central Park West at 104th Street, of 1929-30.

---

[59]   Ernest A. Batchelder (1875-1957) made tiles in the Arts and Crafts tradition from 1912 to 1932, which were sold through showrooms in many U.S. cities. See Norman Karlson, *American Art Tiles: 1876-1941* (New York: Rizzoli, 1998), pp. 157-61. Also Robert Winter, *Batchelder Tilemaker* (Los Angeles: Balcony Press, 1999).

Park Vista, 444 Central Park West, at 104th Street, 1929-30.

Instead of a cornice and flat roof, 444 culminates in a central tower with penthouses and terraces.

The organization of the lower 15 floors of 444 Central Park West still retains much continuity with the rectangular style: there is a one-story base of tawny cast stone, and a shaft of red brick with some random clinker bricks. The decorative details borrow from the Romanesque, and terra cotta pelicans turn up on the fifth and fourteenth floors. In the center bays, molded bricks are stacked to form vertical piers. Spandrels connect the windows from floor to floor to introduce another vertical element. The pier and spandrel pattern has been evident, although not very pronounced, as early as 1915 in 1000 Park Avenue by Roth with Boak's initials on the elevation drawings. Pier and spandrel was used often by Boak & Paris and other architects of the time to emphasize verticality.[60]

At 444 Central Park West, the original windows were multi-pane steel casements. The spacious lobby has extensive unusual tile from the American Encaustic Tile Co. The estimated total cost was $1,125,000. The apartments have three to six rooms, with much individuality - some are duplex, some have wood-burning fireplaces, some have a maid's room - and it is likely that some were custom-designed for the original tenants. The owner, William J. Hanna, had an apartment here in the 1930s.

Boak & Paris designed a building of 19 stories and a penthouse with many setbacks for terraced apartments which was built in 1930-31 by William M. Baumgarten. It is a midblock building at 227 East 57th Street, with a facade and silhouette closely resembling 302 West 12th Street. The materials are red brick and light terra cotta for bandcourses and window surrounds. It was noted in *The New York Times* that "The building is another link toward connecting the midtown section of Fifty-seventh Street with the westward spreading apartment colony

---

[60]   On the use of brick to form piers, see *Skyscraper Style*, p. 54 and footnote; Bletter suggests that this feature derived either from German Gothicizing Expressionist architecture or from American Neogothic skyscrapers such as Cass Gilbert's Woolworth Building (1913), or both.

of Sutton Place."[61] To the south, there was a view all the way to the Chrysler Building.

1930 was the start of a long relationship of Boak & Paris with Arlington C. Hall (1870-1948). Hall's architects from 1900 to 1909 were Neville & Bagge. The most expensive of their nine buildings was the Dorchester at 131 Riverside Drive at 85th Street (1909) which mirrors the adjoining Clarendon at 86th Street and was marketed as a cooperative. Also in 1909, they did the 12-story Cornwall, 255 West 90th Street at Broadway, where Hall made his home.[62] In 1911, Hall switched to Gaetan Ajello, the architect who gave Hyman Paris his start. Hall and Ajello did five apartment houses and the Claremont Theater together from 1911 to 1914.

When Hall next planned an apartment house, in 1928, Ajello was no longer practicing architecture. Hall tried a different architect, Leo Knust, for the 16-story apartment house with cornice, in a simplified Italian Renaissance style, at the northeast corner of Riverside Drive and 104th.

---

61   *The New York Times*, November 11, 1930, Real Estate, p. 1.

62   *The New York Times*, November 16, 1914, p. 12.

Floral terra cotta and window grille on first floor of
315 Riverside Drive, at 104th Street.

Hall owned two other plots on Riverside Drive, one just across 104th
Street from the Knust building and the other at 74th Street, for which
Knust filed plans in 1929. But Hall didn't use Knust for either site; both
were built in 1930-31 to plans by the young firm Boak & Paris.

On the Riverside Drive block from 103rd to 104th, Hall owned
the northern corner while on the adjoining southern corner at 103rd
Street, the Master Building was going up in 1928-29. Louis and Nettie
Horch had commissioned Harvey Wiley Corbett of Helmle, Corbett &
Harrison to design the tallest building on Riverside Drive after Riverside
Church. Andrew Dolkart describes it

> . . . as a 29-story apartment hotel that would incorporate
> the Nicholas Roerich Museum -- including galleries, a library,
> and an auditorium -- on its ground floor. The building is
> among the finest Art Deco high-rise structures in New York
> City. Among its notable features are the patterned brickwork
> that varies from dark to light as the building rises, the dramatic

setbacks and irregular massing of the upper floors, the ornamental crown, and the innovative use of corner windows.[63]

In 1929 Hugh Ferriss explained the significance of this first use in the United States of casement windows at the corner:

> This structure represents more than one innovation which it will be well to remember when it comes to sketching the city of the future. As a matter of fact, what usually attracts the attention of passers-by on the [Riverside] Drive is the unusual placing of the windows -- at the very corners of the structure. Upon some, this produces an uneasy impression -- for the simple reason that their preconceptions of structural strength are based on the masonry structures they have previously seen. To others, this disposition of windows is immediately satisfying -- since they have acquainted themselves with the elements of steel construction and know that this corner treatment is, in steel, structurally sound. The glazed corner is, indeed, justified by the structural fact that it is, in addition, desirable: it provides the corner room with an unusual degree of light and air as well as a sense of spaciousness which will prove surprising to the average city dweller.[64]

Charles C. Savage in the landmarks designation report states that

> Although both residential towers [the Master Apartments and One Fifth Avenue] are girded with the firm's characteristic vertical massing, the Master's heavy corners are pierced by horizontal corner windows, not unlike quoins, and because

---

[63]   Andrew S. Dolkart, *Guide to New York City Landmarks* (New York: John Wiley & Sons, Inc., 1998), p. 124.

[64]   *The Metropolis of Tomorrow*, p. 34. Only the corner windows are casements; most of the Master's windows are sash.

quoining suggests reinforcement, these openings are all the
more striking – a mini-revolution in themselves.[65]

These corner windows provide a strong horizontal element to the
building, but it is horizontality in the service of the vertical: the sides
with these bands of window are like hands holding the center of the
building vertical.

It must have been a challenge for Boak & Paris to design an apartment
house to stand adjacent to the Master Building. Corbett could build
29 stories because it was an apartment hotel for which plans were filed
before the law changed in 1929, while Boak & Paris could build only
19 stories since 315 Riverside Drive was restricted to apartment house
height.[66] Nonetheless the top of 315 Riverside seems to respond to the
Master: Its setbacks start at the level at which the Master has its first
faceted corner, then rise to the level at which the Master has its lowest
terrace. The verticality of the building is clearly defined by treatment of
the outer window stack with decorative terra cotta spandrels carrying up
to the window of the floor above, and molded bricks stacked in piers on
either side of the windows reaching up the entire height of the facades.

Prior to the 1930s, ornament on buildings usually meant applied
ornament. During the Depression, ornament was the creative use of
the construction materials – brick, cast stone and terra cotta. In the
Depression, labor was relatively cheap, while materials were relatively
expensive, so builders could afford to have the bricklayers take the time
to lay brick in patterns, for example.[67]

Boak & Paris considered brick a very expressive material and used
a variety of shapes and colors to produce extremely interesting facades.

---

[65]   Landmarks Preservation Commission Rockefeller Apartments Designation
      Report [LP 1276], New York, City of New York, 1984, prepared by Charles C.
      Savage, p. 4.

[66]   In a striking photograph, the Master Building soars above 315 Riverside Drive;
      Skyscraper Style, plate 19.

[67]   I am indebted to Gregory DeNicola for this observation.

Unusual shades of red-yellow or red-purple were frequently combined. The way in which they manipulated the brick was superb, including molded bricks in stacks as at 315. Bricks could be recessed or protrude from the rest of the wall to provide additional texture. Cast stone was used in the base of 315 (a low base extending only to the first-floor windowsills). The cast stone is made not only in smooth blocks but also blocks with floral designs. The terra cotta has a matte glaze, similar to that of the tan cast stone.

In contrast to the two-story entrances of the Master, which are geometric and German Expressionistic in flavor, the details of 315 are floral, more Parisian. A playful floral motif appears in the lobby and on the exterior in the first floor wrought-iron window grilles, in a witty design of a flowerpot with a blooming flower. The apartments have three to five rooms, with dropped living rooms and fireplaces.

Hall's second Riverside Drive site had quite different neighbors. Planning its demolition, Hall bought a five-story town house at Riverside and 74th Street that had been built in 1895-97 for the banker George H. Macy from plans by C. P. H. Gilbert. It was part of a row of still-extant town houses by Gilbert on the north side of 74th Street, "Florentine in general outline," with many variations.[68] On the south side of 74th Street, in the center of a formal garden, stood the "CHARLES M. SCHWAB MANSION, which lords over the square block from Seventy-third to Seventy-fourth Street. It was designed by Maurice Ebert and is said to have cost more than $2,500,000. The central facade is reminiscent of the chateau of Chenonceaux, and the sides, of the castles of Blois and Azay-le-Rideau."[69]

Since it replaced a town house, 22 Riverside Drive has one of the smallest footprints of any Boak & Paris building, 70 feet on Riverside Drive and 29 feet on West 74th Street. It was built to the maximum legal

---

[68]   Christopher Gray, "An 1896 Row of 11 Town Houses With One Architect," Streetscapes, *The New York Times*, February 3, 2002, Real Estate, p. 7.

[69]   Federal Writers' Project, *New York City Guide* (New York: Works Progress Administration, 1939), p. 286.

height of 19 stories, with only 33 apartments. The West End-Collegiate Historic District Report describes its style as "Eclectic with Gothic and Elizabethan detailing . . . cast stone base; Flemish bond red brick upper floors; setbacks; six-over-one double hung wood sash and corner multi-pane metal casement windows."[70] The materials and color palette are like Broad Park Lodge in White Plains and 444 Central Park West. It has an Arts and Crafts aura, with Batchelder tiles in the lobby.

Probably because they had taken note of the new feature at the Master, at 22 Riverside Drive Boak & Paris used multi-pane steel casement windows at the corner for the first time. The windows however are small and only in one corner so they do not seem to bound the building as the corner windows of the Master seem to do. Casement windows are older than sash windows, and were often used in Tudor Revival houses and apartment buildings of the 1920s and 1930s, including Boak & Paris' Broad Park Lodge. Casement windows permit more ventilation than sash windows: a sash window can never be more than 50 percent open, while a casement window, hinged like a door, can be set 100 percent open, and can be angled to catch a breeze. Other architects who were early to follow Corbett's lead in placing casement windows at the corner were Murchison & Hood, Godley & Fouilhoux in the Beaux-Arts Apartments of 1929-30; Irwin S. Chanin in the Majestic of 1930; and Emery Roth in his first Art Deco building, the Ardsley of 1930-31.[71]

---

[70]   Landmarks Preservation Commission West End-Collegiate Historic District Designation Report, New York, City of New York, 1983, prepared by the Research Staff, Marjorie Pearson, Director; p. 193.

[71]   "Corner-bay Windows" as well as "Drop Living Rooms" were among the new features that explain "why, during a slow market, certain new buildings have become fully occupied at premium rentals while others remain sparsely tenanted, even after rentals are drastically reduced." William J. Farthing, "Style in Apartments as an Effective Renting Factor," *Real Estate Record and Guide*, June 20, 1931. By 1938, the maintenance costs of corner windows were being questioned; as providing less light, no cross ventilation and higher heating costs compared to more conventional windows; Oscar Fisher, "The Effects of Corner Windows on Maintenance Costs," *Real Estate Record and Guide*, March 5, 1938.

Hall lived in the triplex penthouse with conservatory at 22 Riverside Drive until his death in 1948.[72] In 1938 he purchased the adjoining town house at 323 West 74th Street, which had been subdivided into apartments, to assure "light and air for" 22 Riverside Drive.[73]

The Boak & Paris building at 450 West End and 82nd Street (1930-31) was designed for Jacob M. Simon; Boak & Paris eventually did four buildings for the Simon brothers. It replaced the seven-story Carlyle apartment, "reminiscent of the building type of a generation ago," and was "directly opposite the only public school on West End Avenue." With only three apartments per floor, of six or seven rooms each, some with a maid's room, it was built for relatively affluent families on a fairly staid avenue. This 18-story apartment house with setbacks and penthouses is entirely free-standing to maximize circulation of air. In some ways, 450 West End Avenue is conservative, even chaste, without any of the flamboyance of 444 Central Park West and 315 Riverside Drive. No corner casement windows here, and an almost flat facade, with a touch of the Tudor for its penthouse and setbacks. It does, however, include the new feature of the sunken or dropped living room: "All living rooms, 27 by 16 feet in size, are of the new dropped type, with ornamental railing and opening for the full width on the gallery."[74]

Boak & Paris designed another West End Avenue building in 1931, at 336 West End Avenue at 76th Street, opposite 333 West End Avenue, the Hanna building for which Boak had done the elevation drawings in 1925 while still with Roth. The Venetian style of 333 -- rectangular with a flat roof and cornice, and a different design of window on each of the first three floors -- contrasts with 336, a tall building of 19 stories, with its verticality expressed by piers of molded brick, topped by setbacks and terraces and tower. It has variety in the handling of its red brick, giving a textural interest to its facade. Terra cotta is used sparingly on upper floors, perhaps the latest building on which Boak & Paris used this material. Cast stone was a cheaper and more quickly available

---

72   *The New York Times*, December 5, 1948, p. 92.

73   *The New York Times*, October 1, 1938, p. 30.

74   *The New York Times*, January 25, 1931, Real Estate, p. 31.

material, which could be made to resemble many natural stones, and even molded like terra cotta. In place of window surrounds, which would have been in light terra cotta or cast stone, there is machicolation in brick at the fourth, fourteenth and sixteenth floor levels.

The site had formerly been occupied by the 12-story Lombardi, erected only 20 years prior and solidly built, "but owing to the difficulty of renting its large suites, the building was torn down last fall. The present house with two to four-room apartments is better adapted to modern needs." This building for Frank Sox was regarded as one of the "only two high-grade apartment houses" built in 1932 between 59th and 110th Streets; the other is 501 West 113th Street by George F. Pelham.[75] Like 450 West End Avenue, 336 does not jar the calm of West End Avenue. The lobby retains many elegant classical details.

When Arlington Hall was finishing 22 and 315 Riverside Drive in June 1931 for October occupancy, he expressed satisfaction with the renting experience the previous year at the Knust-designed building on the northeast corner of Riverside Drive and 104th Street: 124 apartments fully rented. In fact, "our satisfactory renting experience has led us to plan another apartment house at the south corner of Central Park West and 105th Street"[76] -- just north of William J. Hanna's 444 Central Park West, where Hanna had planned in 1929 to erect a twin to 444 Central Park West.[77] But like Hanna, Hall did not build there; the nineteenth-century French flats stand to this day.

The young new firm was extremely busy from its launch in 1927 until 1931. These years were not without troubles, however. Russell Boak and Hyman Paris had formed Pariboke Realty Corp. as owner and contractor for their Broad Park Lodge in White Plains. According to notices in The New York Times in 1929 to 1931, there were judgments filed against the Pariboke Realty Corp. and/or against them individually by a variety of creditors, including electrical suppliers, mantel and grate

---

75   *The New York Times*, April 17, 1932, Real Estate, p. 1.

76   *The New York Times*, June 7, 1931, Real Estate, p. 6.

77   *The New York Times*, January 5, 1930.

works, and painters and decorators. The amounts ranged from $200 to nearly $12,000, and the claims were filed mainly in New York County (Manhattan), Westchester, Queens, Brooklyn and the Bronx. The locations of the building sites are not given, so it is possible, but probably unlikely, that all of these claims relate only to Broad Park Lodge.

It is not usual for architects to be builders as well, and Boak and Paris may have found it burdensome.[78]

It is considered that 1932-33 was the depth of the Depression and the pace of residential construction nearly halted completely. So it is not surprising that Hall's next commission for Boak & Paris was not residential.

---

[78] In 1937, Hyman Paris and Russell Boak filed individually for bankruptcy as builders; see Chapter 5.

CHAPTER 3

Arlington C. Hall: Cars and Theaters

Arlington C. Hall was ahead of his times in two things: he had the Claremont Theatre specifically designed to show "photoplays" and he was an early owner of a motor car. A story in *The New York Times* in 1914 links his two interests:

60 SHOTS IN AUTO CHASE
Police in Three Speeding Cars
Finally Overhaul Thieves.

Martin Moran, 19, of 176 East 127th Street; Jerry Curtin, 22, of 216 East 123rd Street, and Fred Schweers, 25, of 224 East 125th Street, were arrested early yesterday morning after being chased by the police several miles through the streets of Harlem. The prisoners were in a stolen automobile with three others who escaped. More than sixty shots were fired by pursued and pursuers in the chase. Magistrate Murphy in the Harlem Court held the three for trial on complaint of Arlington C. Hall, a real estate dealer of 255 West Ninetieth Street.

Mr. Hall said that when his son Paul came out of a theatre at 135th Street and Broadway he saw six men driving his father's car away. Paul Hall jumped into his own machine with his father's chauffeur, Frank Watson, and gave chase. The stolen machine raced down Broadway at forty-five miles an hour, and at 102nd Street Hall stopped to take on Policeman Sewall of the West 100th Street Station, who started shooting at the tires of the car ahead.

At 110th Street and Fifth Avenue Policeman McDonald of the East 126th Street Station fired six shots and exploded a tire. The car swerved and the men turned their guns on McDonald, one bullet tearing through his coat.

At 120th Street the stolen car slowed down and three men jumped out, taking two new tires with them, and at 121st Street it stopped and the other three men were arrested.[79]

It seems remarkable that in 1914 the Hall family owned not just one, but two, cars, and that the police would engage in a shoot-out to catch car thieves.

The theater from which this chase started was the Claremont, one of the first structures built specifically to show motion pictures.

---

[79] *The New York Times*, November 16, 1914, p. 12.

The Claremont Theater, 3320 Broadway at West 135th Street,
opened in 1914. It was designed by Gaetan Ajello for Arlington C. and
Harvey M. Hall. When movies became "talkies," the old theater was
converted in 1933 into an automobile showroom,
with a two-story addition to the south, designed by Boak & Paris.

Matthew A. Postal wrote in the designation report that the
Claremont, built in 1913-14, was

> commissioned by Arlington C. Hall and Harvey M.
> Hall of the Wayside Realty Company, it was designed in
> the neo-Renaissance style by Gaetano Ajello, an architect
> best-known for apartment buildings on Manhattan's Upper
> West Side. The building has three distinct fronts, including
> a clipped corner facade where the auditorium's entrance was
> originally located. This distinctive arrangement enhanced
> the theater's visibility and increased the amount of retail
> space. The corner, consequently, received the most elaborate

decorative treatment and is embellished with an elegant low relief depicting an early motion picture camera set on a tripod. In 1915 Thomas Edison produced a short film in which the theater's entrance is prominently featured. Filmed from across Broadway, it depicts groups of men, women, and children exiting the building. The second floor accommodated a large restaurant and ballroom, known under such names as the Broadway-Claremont or Clarendon Restaurant, and later, the Royal Palms Ballroom and Roof Garden. Until the early years of Depression, area residents gathered here to eat, drink, and dance.[80]

In only a few years, the Claremont became out of date. In 1927, "photoplays" were transformed into "talkies" when *The Jazz Singer* starring Al Jolson came out. Hall's response was to build a new movie theater farther down on Broadway and almost simultaneously change the Claremont Theater into an automobile showroom. Boak & Paris did both jobs for Hall. The designation report states that

> Beginning in the late 1920s, the owner began to lease the retail spaces to automobile-related businesses, including Desoto, Shur Motor Company, Level Auto & Radio Company, and Goodrich tires. The *New York Times* reported in August 1933 that the area had become an "automobile centre" and that the "old Claremont Theatre property" was being remodeled to serve as a large automobile showroom and service station. Though hardly old in terms of years, by 1930 audience expectations had greatly changed. Movie palaces, now outfitted with increasingly exotic decoration and sound, must have made aging pioneers like the Claremont seem dated and obsolete.

> During 1933-34 a three-story orange brick addition by the architects Boak & Paris was erected at the south end of

---

[80]   Landmarks Preservation Commission Claremont Theater Designation Report [LP-2198], New York, City of New York, 2006, prepared by Matthew A. Postal, p. 1.

the parcel and the original Ajello building, except for the interiors, was retained.[81]

When Hall considered building a new theater, he must have known how Boak & Paris had updated the Variety Photo Plays Theater at 110 Third Avenue near 14th Street (demolished). Christopher Gray wrote that

> In 1930, a balcony seating 150 and a new lobby were installed by the architects Boak & Paris, who also made over the 1923 marquee. The lobby is nondescript neo-Renaissance and it is the marquee that has made the theater special, at least to modern eyes. Boak & Paris did not change the Eckman marquee's underside, a coffered field with regularly spaced bulbs, but did add a zigzag Art Deco fascia in enameled metal and neon lighting. The fascia gives the theater's, rather than the show's, name and recalls the period when movies were more of a generic product. The lights buzzing on the underside of the marquee, when they were on, enveloped the passerby in a warm, glowing field. People going past the theater, even in the daytime, got a whiff of vintage celluloid, and at night it was intoxicating.[82]

Hall's new theater was the Midtown Theater, on Broadway between 99th and 100th Streets, for which plans were first filed in 1931, and which was built in 1932-33.

---

[81] Ibid., p. 5.

[82] Christopher Gray, *Changing New York: The Architectural Scene* (New York: Dover Publications, 1992), p. 98.

The Midtown (now the Metro) Theater,
designed by Boak & Paris for A. C. and H. M. Hall,
2626 Broadway, between 99th and 100th Streets, opened in 1933.

Boak & Paris used lights on the underside of the marquee at the Midtown, to create the similar effect as at the Variety. But it is the facade above the marquee that makes the Midtown stand out, as noted in the report designating it a New York City landmark:

> The most notable feature of the theater's facade is the tripartite decorative terra-cotta wall above the marquee. The central section is composed of rectangular panels of black terra cotta, flanked by slightly projecting black terra-cotta pilasters outlined in maroon terra cotta, which curve at the top, extending above the wall . . . In the center of the black terra-cotta section is a vertical accent consisting of banded aluminum bars, which also extend above the wall in a triangular pattern. This is interrupted by a large, circular, glazed terra-cotta medallion, set within an aluminum frame, which contains off-white and beige bas-relief stylized figures holding gray and blue theatrical-mask disks which represent comedy and tragedy, symbolic of the building's function . . .[83]

Stern, Gilmartin and Mellins regard the Midtown as

> stylishly Modernist. The stadium-type auditorium was unified by a band of Modern Classical floral ornament carved in low relief that ran down the center of the ceiling toward the top of the screen. Niches on either side contained statues of nude women holding alabaster dishes that glowed with light.[84]

---

[83] Landmarks Preservation Commission Midtown Theater (now Metro Theater) Designation Report, [LP-1615], New York, City of New York, 1989, prepared by Lynne D. Marthey, pp.5-6.

[84] Robert A. M. Stern, Gregory Gilmartin and Thomas Mellins, *New York 1930: Architecture and Urbanism Between the Two World Wars* (New York: Rizzoli International Publications, Inc.), 1987, p. 264.

The interior of the Midtown Theater,
with its stadium-type seating before it was "twinned" in 1986.

It is as if the two nude figures on the facade had walked inside to grace the side aisles, although looking a little more chaste.

In 1933, Boak & Paris did alterations to another movie theater at Broadway and 89th Street, adding a "new front & marquee, rearrange seating & partitions, projection booth, plumbing, heating $30,000." Then known as the Yorktown Theater, Dan Talbot renamed it the New Yorker (demolished) when he took it over in 1962. As reported in *The New York Times*,

> In "Annie Hall," Woody Allen dragged Diane Keaton there to see "The Sorrow and the Pity." . . .

> [In 1982, Talbot] acquired the lease to the Metro, a onetime porn theater known as the Midtown. "It was a filthy mess," he said. "A lot of whisky bottles, torn seats, totally

rundown. But I got some lights and got my architect in there, and it turns out this theater was an architectural gem."[85]

This movie theater renamed the Metro is Boak & Paris' only individually landmarked building, and their most-cited work.[86] In his *Guide to New York City Landmarks*, Andrew Dolkart wrote that

> In the 1920s and 1930s, Broadway on the Upper West Side was lined with neighborhood movie theaters. The Art Deco Midtown is not only one of the few still functioning, but it also has one of the finest theater facades in New York. The street front is clad entirely in colored terra cotta, primarily beige and black. The focus of the design is a medallion with a bas-relief of figures and masks representing comedy and tragedy.[87]

The Metro was managed by Clearview Cinemas until an abrupt close in 2003. The owner Albert Bialek then leased it to Peter H. Elson, who put a reported $450,000 into renovations of what he called "the Embassy's New Metro Twin." However, business was slow perhaps because Elson's taste in movies was obscure. It was speculated in *The New York Times*

> For Mr. Elson there is still some hope. Two residential high-rises with family-size apartments will soon be built on the block, which could perhaps bring more business.

[85]   "Fade to Black," *The New York Times*, April 6, 2003, Section 14, p. 9.

[86]   *Skyscraper Style*, text p. 87, plate 100. Stern, Gilmartin and Mellins, *New York 1930*, text p. 264, illustrations p. 257. Carla Breeze, *New York Deco* (New York: Rizzoli, 1993), illustration, pp. 60-61. Susan Tunick, *Terra-Cotta Skyline: New York's Architectural Ornament* (New York: Princeton Architectural Press, 1997), illustration, p. 97.

[87]   *Guide to New York City Landmarks*, 2nd edition, p. 124.

"If we make it that long," he said.[88]

He didn't. The noise of the construction of Ariel East and West on Broadway between 99th and 100th Streets may have contributed to the shuttering of the Metro as a movie theater. Although it had been "twinned" into upper and lower theaters in 1986, the Metro retained its distinctive ceiling and the naked ladies in the niches until 2006 when the interior was gutted in hopes of renting it as a retail store. This was legal because only the exterior, not the interior, of the Metro is protected by landmarking.

Alamo Drafthouse Cinema, a chain based in Austin, Texas, announced in 2012 plans to open a movie house in New York, and hoisted a banner on the Metro: "Coming in 2014 – Drafthouse Cinema ALAMO." But in October 2013, Alamo posted the information on its website that "we cannot see this particular location as sustainable under the current conditions."[89] So once again, the future of this landmark is unknown.

*   *   *

In 1933 the pressing question for Boak & Paris was whether the Depression would prevent them from ever doing apartment buildings again. Hall had them design an office for him by remodeling a town house at 143 West 72nd Street in 1935.

---

[88] Jeff Vandam, "Braced Once More For a Last Picture Show," *The New York Times*, September 4, 2005, CY, p. 6.

[89] *The New York Times*, October 21, 2013, p. C3.

In 1935, Boak & Paris renovated 143 West 72nd Street,
between Amsterdam and Columbus Avenues,
to serve as an office for the Halls.

But Hall was not the one who gave them the opportunity to do their
next apartment building. That man was Samuel Minskoff.

CHAPTER 4

Sam Minskoff: The Nadir of the Depression and the Uptick in 1936

Sam Minskoff built only one more building with Emery Roth after Russell Boak and Hyman Paris had left the firm, and it is possible that the designs may have been in preparation even before the two had left. Roth's biographer Ruttenbaum wrote that the luxury building at 480 Park Avenue at 58ᵗʰ Street

> . . . was constructed in 1928-29 of buff brick and limestone with terra-cotta ornament executed in the Italian Renaissance revival style. Roth did not endow it with the same boxy appearance he gave the previous Minskoff buildings; instead, the upper floors were stepped back in a rather asymmetrical manner that resembles adobe pueblos of the southwest United States. This picturesque composition is crowned by a water tower clothed in a luxuriant skin of Renaissance details.

> Advertised to prospective tenants as "a home of social distinction," 480 Park Avenue is a 19-story building consisting of a wide range of apartment sizes, from three to thirteen rooms. They were arranged on a foyer plan as both simplex and duplex suites, and they offered their tenants

luxurious amenities that included high ceilings, wood-burning fireplaces and large terraces.[90]

It opened for occupancy in November 1929, just after the stock market crash of October 29, 1929; it may have been slow to become fully rented.[91]

After that, Sam Minskoff took a breather from building in Manhattan. When he resumed building apartment houses in 1931, it was in the Bronx, two six-story non-fireproof tenements, and he didn't return to Emery Roth. Instead he used the young firm of Boak & Paris, who were probably cheaper. Going forward, Minskoff was their most frequent client.

The two 1931 buildings for Minskoff on Gun Hill Road in the Bronx present an interesting contrast. They have many similarities: each is six stories with a flat roof and about the same overall dimensions; each had an estimated cost of $150,000, and nearly the same number of units. Where they differ is in their facades: while both use a light cream brick, the building east of Putnam Place is traditional with cartouches and terra cotta window enframements; the one west of Putnam Place has corner casement windows and its ornament is not terra cotta, but created by the use of darker colored brick in the spandrels. Under the corner windows, there are horizontal bands of the darker brick, while in the spandrels that form vertical columns with their windows, the contrasting brick runs vertically. Where did this design come from?

---

[90]   *Mansions in the Clouds*, pp. 72-73.

[91]   In his *Autobiographical Notes* (pp. 305-07), Roth wrote that in one building he disputed the charges of "a plumbing contractor"; this man was also a speculative builder who then asked Roth to design for him if he would fight as hard for him as he had against him in the prior building. Roth said they did six or seven buildings over ten years. "We parted over a contention involving a comparatively trifling amount of money." This is a deliberate put-down of Minskoff: in his *Notes*, Roth usually identifies his clients, and the record shows that the firm did 11 buildings for Minskoff, not just six or seven.

One of the most prolific and influential architects of the Grand Concourse and elsewhere in the Bronx and upper Manhattan was Horace Ginsberg (later Ginsbern). Marvin Fine was the designer of the exteriors of Ginsberg's apartment buildings, including the Park Plaza at 1005 Jerome Avenue near 164th Street (1929-31) and Noonan Plaza at 168th Street and Nelson Avenue (1931). Anthony Robins interviewed Fine and comments that

> Its striking modernistic effect [of Park Plaza] derives from the arrangement of the windows in vertical shafts of windows and recessed spandrels . . .

> [Raymond] Hood's great striped 1929 headquarters for the Daily News replaced Fine's office. Moving across the street, he then watched the Daily News Building rise. Fine "met Raymond Hood . . . his style made me design all of these apartment buildings with the vertical shafts" of recessed windows and spandrels so typical of the modernistic buildings of the late 1920s and 1930s . . . "And all up the Concourse you'll see the buildings we designed, with the colored brick, change of brick in between spandrels . . . That I got directly from him."[92]

In 1931 Russell Boak and Hyman Paris would have known both the Daily News building, because their offices were then at 11 West 42nd Street, and the Ginsbern-Fine buildings in the Bronx, because the Gun Hill Road buildings for Minskoff are only a few blocks away. Their Gun Hill Road building differs from Ginsbern-Fine buildings because Boak & Paris used a slightly lighter color in the horizontal bands of accent brick.

In their contrasting Gun Hill Road buildings, it is as if Boak & Paris posed the question to Sam Minskoff, do you want Traditional or

---

[92] [Anthony Robins], *Everyday Masterpieces: Memory & Modernity: a study of an international vernacular architecture between the two world wars*, by Joselita Raspi Serra, Françoise Astorg Bollack and Tom Killian (Modena, Edizioni Panini, 1988), p. 217.

Modern? Do you want to look back to the 1920s or to look up- to-date? For whatever reason – and it may have had to do with how well the buildings rented - from then on, the buildings they designed for Minskoff were decidedly Modern.

As recounted earlier, the Depression slowed the pace of their work greatly in 1931 to 1933 – only one Manhattan apartment house (336 West End Avenue), a movie theater, alterations. The small apartment house at 3 East 66th Street (1933-34) for Minskoff was heralded as "a new star up in the sky . . . the first [apartment building] to be built in more months than the building trades care to think about."

3 East 66th Street, between Fifth and Madison Avenues, 1933-34.

Minskoff said

> There is a very marked trend toward smaller and
> smarter apartments. No matter how skillfully remodeling is
> undertaken, the results can never equal dwellings which are
> built to the purpose. The small apartment requires planning
> of a specialized nature if its facilities are to be complete.
> We feel that, in this new house, we have provided for a
> maximum of comfort and liveability without the sacrifice of
> any efficient requisite.[93]

Stern, Gilmartin and Mellins in *New York 1930* single out this little
building as one of the finest examples of Modern Classical design: "Boak
& Paris's vertically striated, 12-story brick and stone building at 3 East
Sixty-sixth Street of 1933-34 offered the faintly theatrical suggestion of
a curtain."[94] The two-story base is fluted, with sash window frames in
black, while the light brick shaft has window frames in white. Between
the eighth and ninth floors, there is a stringcourse, and the parapet has a
wrought iron railing. There were nineteen apartments of two and three
rooms. The entrance lobby was in modern Empire style. It is small –
only 34 by 80 feet – and cost only $100,000.

The building is on the site of the last home of Ulysses S. Grant,
the Civil War General and 18th President of the United States, where
"he spent his last months writing his 'Personal Memoirs,'" according
to a plaque placed on the building by the New York Community Trust.

In 1934, the Minskoff-Boak & Paris team erected a six-story
tenement of red brick and cast stone at 405 East 72nd Street. Up to this
height, buildings could be non-fireproof, and this kept the estimated
cost to $125,000. The facade has some decorative elements often found
in later Boak & Paris buildings: symmetry on the two sides of the
entrance; an anchoring stringcourse above the first story supporting
a pier of molded brick that rises to an ornament above the top floor.

---

93   *The Skyscraper Times*, May 1934, p. 57.

94   *New York 1930*, p. 398. The building is actually ten stories (nine plus penthouse).

The materials are ones they used repeatedly, common red brick and limestone or cast stone (earlier sometimes terra cotta). Its lobby shows design features they often used: molded plaster in the ceiling subtly painted, terrazzo floor, here in black and white checkerboard.

For many architects, alterations can be bread-and-butter work, and Boak & Paris did their share of alterations. In 1878 James E. Ware designed four row houses on East 64th Street, Nos. 128 to 134. Only 128 retains its original facade, while 130 was given a mesh screen by Edward Durrell Stone when it was his residence. On 132 and 134, Boak & Paris removed the stoop, cornice and other ornament, and gave a stuccoed facade to the two houses, which were subdivided into apartments in 1934. At 217 East 61st Street, their work was to rearrange stairs and bathrooms, and again the stoop was removed in 1935.

The year 1936 marked a pick-up in new construction of apartment houses in New York City. Probably the most publicity concerned the Rockefeller Apartments designed by Harrison & Fouilhoux. The two buildings at 17 West 54th Street and 24 West 55th Street, connected by an interior garden, were meant for executives working at Rockefeller Center. While they were still under construction, the Rockefeller Apartments were included in a photo essay about "Apartment House Design" in *Real Estate Record* – and on the facing page was shown the Boak & Paris building at 50 East 78th Street, at a similar stage in construction.[95] And on their completion, these two buildings were again featured in 1937 issues of *Architectural Forum* and *Real Estate Record*.[96]

In the opinion of Stern, Gilmartin and Mellins, "The firm's most sophisticated Modernist statement was an apartment house at 50 East Seventy-eighth Street of 1936, in which casement corner windows were incorporated into a fundamentally Classical limestone and brick composition."[97]

---

[95] *Real Estate Record*, August 15, 1936, Rockefeller, p. 26; 50 East 78th St., p. 27.

[96] *Architectural Forum*, May 1937, pp. 397 ff. *Real Estate Record*, September 4, 1937, pp. 21-34.

[97] *New York 1930*, pp. 398-99.

50 East 78th Street, between Madison and Park Avenues, 1936.

The facade is primarily red brick. Rather than window surrounds on just one level, the light-colored stone rises from the third to the tenth floor. Some of the classical references included fluting in the base, a Greek key design in the sill at the third floor level and an urn at the top of this wide pilaster.

The article in *Architectural Forum* for May 1937 explains how the economy drove its design:

This building is located in a residential neighborhood in New York where small apartments are in active demand. Building for investment rather than quick resale influenced both plan and construction, and minimum upkeep and slow obsolescence became important factors. In designing the building the type of apartments considered most rentable were first worked out [two to four rooms], then costs were estimated, and final decisions as to materials and exterior design were made on the basis of these controlling elements. The setbacks on the street facade were made to give the rooms another exposure; by the use of corner windows on a narrow street the view is considerably enlarged. The interiors show the continued trend toward greater simplicity in design. The dropped living room, illustrated on the facing page, is a feature which has become extremely popular in New York during the past few years, and its use is rapidly being extended to less expensive apartments.[98]

An article in *The New York Times* is headed "West Side Realty Showing Recovery," and summarizes activity in 1936:

West Side brokers and owners have just closed a year with more tangible evidence of prosperity than they have experienced since the advent of the depression period seven years ago.

The situation for 1937 looks even brighter and there is more confidence and hopefulness in real estate circles throughout that great home area west of Central Park all the way from Fifty-ninth Street northward to Washington Heights and the Dyckman and Inwood sections at the extreme end of Manhattan Island . . .

---

[98] *Architectural Forum*, May 1937, pp. 412-13. The article is illustrated with photos, floor plans and a construction outline listing materials. There is good reason to believe that they learned these design and planning principles from Emery Roth; see *Mansions in the Clouds*, pp. 181-85.

Victor M. Earle of the Earle & Calhoun firm says that one cause for optimism is the fact that rents are likely to rise to a point where landlords may enjoy a small income.

"One of the best signs of the past year," he says, "has been the elimination of defaulting tenants. In 1931 and 1932 this item was a very large one, but with 1933 it began to decline. Another good sign is in the change of attitude of the tenants who no longer demand a drastic cut in rents with elaborate renovations and decorations.

"Tenants who have been doubling up and living in crowded quarters are beginning to come into the market and look for permanent space. The fact of these better conditions will not be felt until next October, when leases expire and an early season for renting is looked for. Real estate conditions must improve when general conditions and all other lines have improved."[99]

Of the eleven apartment houses cited in this article, five are by Boak & Paris: 336 West End Avenue (1931-32); 5 Riverside Drive (1936-37); 100 Riverside Drive (1937-38); 5 West 86th Street (1937-38); and 250 Cabrini Boulevard (1936). Also listed are three by H. I. Feldman – 565 West End Avenue (1937), 4566 Broadway (1936), and 587 West 214th Street (1937). Three other architects are cited with one each: 411 West End Avenue by George Fred Pelham II (1936); 725 West 184th Street, Samson Becker (1936); and 4690 Broadway, [Tryon Gardens], Sugarman & Berger (1936).[100]

Construction of apartment buildings in Washington Heights was spurred by the completion of the Independent Subway System (IND) to 207th Street and Broadway and the opening of the George Washington

---

[99]   *The New York Times*, January 31, 1937, Real Estate, p. 1.

[100] Another sign of the pick-up in construction is the second wave of construction on the Grand Concourse in the Bronx, 1935-41; the first wave had been in the 1920s.

Bridge. On the same day that plans for 50 East 78th Street were filed, February 24, 1936, Leo Minskoff – Sam's oldest son – filed plans for a six-story tenement at 77 Cooper Street, with stores in its 207th Street front. Leo used his father's architects Boak & Paris.

Sam Minskoff had two Boak & Paris buildings uptown, which dominate the irregular intersection of West 187th Street, Cabrini Boulevard (then known as Northern Boulevard) and Pinehurst Avenue. When approached up the hill from Fort Washington Avenue, 250 Cabrini Boulevard (1936) seems to cut off West 187th Street (actually 187th Street jogs slightly to the north).

250 Cabrini Boulevard, and West 187th Street, 1936.

A totally free-standing building, it fronts on three streets, Cabrini Boulevard on the east, 187th Street on the north, and Chittenden Avenue on the west. All west-facing apartments and many north- and south-facing apartments have views of the Hudson River. In this neighborhood the property lines are derived from old farm boundaries, with the later overlay of streets, so this building is wider on Chittenden than on Cabrini. Consequently, the south (rear) wall is not perpendicular to the adjoining walls. In addition, 187th Street slopes down to the west, so the building has eight stories on Cabrini and nine on Chittenden.

On the Cabrini facade, a molded brick pier ascends from a horizontal bracket of light-colored cast stone under the two center windows of the second floor to a palmette ornament at the level of the coping. This element is repeated three times on the 187th Street facade and twice on the Chittenden facade. Like 50 East 78th, 250 Cabrini has recesses, front and rear; this gives 250 Cabrini eight, not four corners, all with corner windows. While 50 East 78th Street had only casement windows, 250 Cabrini had a combination of multi-pane steel casement windows on the corners and narrower sash windows, three over three.

A photo from about 1940 shows a sign saying "Now Leasing 2, 2-1/2, 3, 3-1/2, 4, 4-1/2."[101] The wrought iron entry doors have a floral motif, carried over into the ceiling moldings in the lobby.

As at 50 East 78th Street and other of their buildings, there was a roof deck for all tenants. Long-time tenants remember a roof garden, and, to rinse off after gardening or sun bathing, residents could shower on each landing of the internal fire stairs. (Since it is taller than six stories, it is considered a fireproof building; buildings of six or fewer stories have external fire escapes.) These older residents also remember that apartments had screen doors so that the main doors could be open, allowing cross breezes. And they recall that they called some of their neighbors "aunt" and "uncle" even if they were not family members.

The other Boak & Paris building for Minskoff at this intersection is 255 Cabrini (1936-37), at the northern terminus of Pinehurst Avenue.

---

[101]   Tax photo 1940, Collections of the Municipal Archives of the City of New York.

255 Cabrini Boulevard, and West 187th Street, 1936-37.

Also irregularly shaped, its entrance is on the diagonal cutting off the corner of 187th Street and Cabrini. The entrance is very similar to the contemporary 5 Riverside Drive: they share a broken pediment containing an urn, a band with the Greek key motif and other details. 255 Cabrini is eight stories, matching the Cabrini front of 250. The motifs used in the cast stone are classical -- Grecian urns are set into the coping at the roof, Roman stele sit atop a two-window stack. 255 appears, and is, more bulky than 250, but the red brick and light cast stone are the same. 255 has some shallow bay windows, blunting much of the verticality that is usually so strong in Boak & Paris buildings of these years.[102]

---

[102] Adjacent to 255 Cabrini, Boak & Paris designed a one-story taxpayer for the corner of West 187th Street and Fort Washington Avenue. Several of the storefronts are intact with cast stone trim, but a fire destroyed the eastern end of this structure, and the replacement lacks the cast stone designs.

An article in *The New York Times* calls 250 Cabrini a "tall edifice"; at eight stories, it is tall only in the context of the surrounding neighborhood where most apartment houses are five or six stories.[103] The Minskoff buildings are relatively short at six to eleven stories. The land on which these buildings stand would have been relatively cheap, being midblock on side streets or in outlying neighborhoods. Although these buildings have flat roofs, Boak & Paris did not return to the heavy cornices of the earlier rectangular apartment buildings. Interest is given to the skyline by interrupting masonry parapets with sections of wrought iron railings or cast stone urns.

According to Gertrude Sklar Bell, who worked for the architects from 1937 to early 1942, "Boak & Paris would have gone out of business if it weren't for Sam Minskoff, who seemed to have money when others didn't."[104]

Boak & Paris designed 99 Marble Hill Avenue at 228th Street for Sidney J. Bernstein (1936-37). With its slope, it is six stories on the south and seven stories on the north. With its red brick piers, cast stone entrance, and corner casement windows, it strongly resembles other Boak & Paris buildings of that year.

One of their most noticed buildings rose at the corner of 73rd Street and Riverside Drive. Until the early 1930s, the tracks of the New York Central Railroad were open along the shoreline of the Hudson River. "Between 1934 and 1937 a plan known as the West Side Improvement was executed along the riverfront under the guidance of Robert Moses . . . Most of the labor was provided by relief workers, who enclosed the railroad tracks and built a promenade over them and added a lower level on landfill for athletic fields and tennis courts."[105] This improved the view from Riverside Drive.

---

[103]   *The New York Times*, June 21, 1936.

[104]   Gertrude Sklar Bell, interview by the author July 27, 2001.

[105]   Kenneth T. Jackson, ed., *The Encyclopedia of New York*, Second edition (New York: Yale University Press, 2010), "Riverside Park," p. 1109.

Five Riverside Drive at 73rd Street(1936-37) rises 19 stories plus penthouse, with setbacks and terraces on the 17th to 19th stories.

5 Riverside Drive, and West 73rd Street, 1936-37.

The one-story base is of limestone, and in its red brick facade are the central vertical elements of piers and spandrels. All windows were steel casements. *The New York Times* reports that the exterior is of "modern classic" design.[106] Like their buildings designed in the same years, there

---

106   *The New York Times*, October 6, 1936.

are elements borrowed from the Greeks and Romans: the Greek key, the broken pediment with urn, crossed arrows. The front on Riverside Drive appears to be symmetrical and balanced (in fact there is one more bay on its south half). Like other Boak & Paris buildings, it has an irregular footprint, as Riverside Drive and 73rd Street meet at an acute angle. Since the block from 73rd to 74th Streets on the drive was occupied by the extensive gardens of the Schwab mansion, 5 Riverside Drive had a view of 22 Riverside Drive (Boak & Paris, 1930-31).[107]

Five Riverside Drive was featured in *Real Estate Record* and *Architectural Record*, both with photos and layout plans.[108] Rents are given as $47 per room per month. To appeal to affluent families, some apartments have three bedrooms and there are some maids' rooms. *Pencil Points* for June 1938 presented comparative detail by drawings and a photo of its revolving door on the drive: "Designed by Boak & Paris, it was built by Simon Bros., who recently reported its purchase by the New York Protestant Episcopal Public Schools as an investment."[109] Although no address is given, it is clearly recognizable as 5 Riverside.

---

[107]   The Schwab mansion was demolished in 1948, and replaced by Schwab House, designed by Sylvan Bien in 1949. Schwab House almost completely fills its lot, so it is wider than the flanking Boak & Paris buildings, but slightly shorter at 18 stories plus penthouse. Like its two Boak & Paris neighbors, Schwab House is in red brick.

[108]   *Real Estate Record*, September 4, 1937, pp. 30-31, with photos and floor plans. *Architectural Record*, October 1937, pp. 146-47 with exterior photo, Schedule of Equipment and Materials, and floor plans of first, typical, 17th and 18th, 19th and penthouse floors.

[109]   *Pencil Points*, June 1938, p. 392.

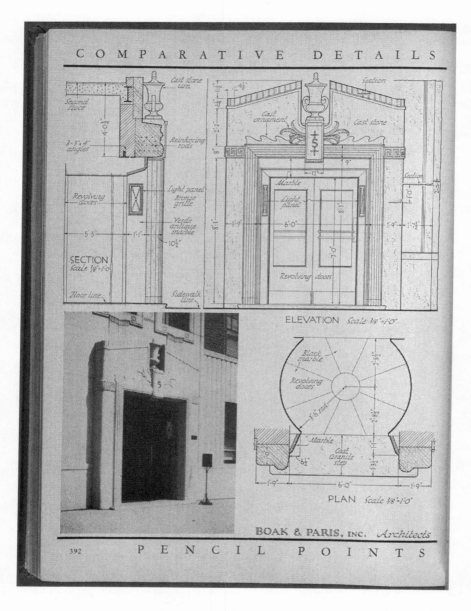

Detail of entrance to 5 Riverside Drive, 1936-37.

The real estate exchange conducted while the building was still under construction was complex: the headlines in *The New York Times* read "Episcopalians Get 20-Story Apartment Structure at 73rd St. as an

Investment; Deal Involves $2,500,000; 30 Properties in Manhattan and Bronx Turned Over to Builders in Exchange."[110] Most of the owners who engaged Boak & Paris built for their own accounts – they would manage their buildings even after completion, so costs of maintenance were more important than initial skimping on materials and labor. While the Simon brothers sold this building before the completion of construction, the same ethic must have prevailed because the schools bought 5 Riverside Drive as an investment.

Just two months after the completion of 5 Riverside Drive, Boak & Paris filed plans for 100 Riverside Drive (1937-38) for "Natoma Estates, a syndicate headed by Simon Bros . . . decorations will be by Elsie de Wolfe, Inc."[111] These two Simon buildings differ in the angle at which the side street meets the drive: 100 Riverside Drive on the northeast corner with 82nd Street has an obtuse angle, while 5 Riverside Drive on the southeast corner of 73rd has an acute angle. Both are 19 stories tall, including setbacks and terraces. Like 5 Riverside, 100 Riverside has a one-story limestone base and red brick facade with piers, but not the spandrels. Each of its facades appear symmetrical and balanced. The windows were steel casement throughout.

To build 100 Riverside Drive, it was necessary to demolish the smallest house ever built on Riverside Drive - three stories, eight rooms. It had been built only six years before "to comply with restrictions in the deed specifying that a private home must be built there before it could be used for other purposes."[112]

Five West 86th Street (1937-38) replaced the town house of "Diamond Jim" Brady.

---

[110] *The New York Times*, March 11, 1937.

[111] *The New York Times*, February 6, 1938, Real Estate, p. 4. The lobby has since been redecorated.

[112] *The New York Times*, January 31, 1937, Real Estate p. 9.

5 West 86th Street, between Central Park West
and Columbus Avenue, 1937-38.

The owner was 5 West 86th Street Corp., headed by Irving Broff.[113]
Boak & Paris used a tawny tan brick rather than their more usual red
brick; a similar tan brick is used in the immediately-adjacent Society
for Advancement of Judaism (1938, Albert Goldhammer, architect).
The building rises 19 stories with setbacks, terraces and penthouse. It is
almost symmetrical with a strong vertical pier rising from the two-story
cast stone base. It retains its steel casement windows. At the height of
the top of the synagogue, there is a beltcourse, with corner casement

---

[113]   *The New York Times*, February 14, 1937, Real Estate, p. 1.

windows above that. There are dropped living rooms. The report on the Upper West Side Historic District describes its style as Moderne.[114]

Boak & Paris designed 110 East 87th Street (1937) for Sidney Bernstein in a more conservative Tudor style.

110 East 87th Street, between Park and Lexington Avenues, 1937.

114 Landmarks Preservation Commission Upper West Side Historic District Designation Report [LP-1647], New York, City of New York, 1990, prepared by Research Department, Marjorie Pearson, Director, Project/Research Coordination, Jay Shockley, Deputy Director of Research, vol. 3, p. 583.

It is a midblock building of 11 stories plus penthouse. The most striking feature of this very symmetrical building is its central three-window stack, with light cast stone spandrels contrasting with the red brick. The windows are multipane steel casements; corner windows were possible only at the setback. At the same time, Bernstein had another building nearing completion at 231 East 76th Street by Sugarman & Berger, in a distinctly Modern style, with corner casement windows. "While the two buildings were designed by different architects, both were laid out with a view of 'combining compactness of fewer rooms with the spaciousness of larger units,' according to the sponsors."[115]

Sam Minskoff commissioned 152 East 94th Street (1937), a 12-story building to house 110 families, considerably larger than any others he commissioned from Boak & Paris in the 1930s. Located midblock, it is quite wide. Red brick and cast stone are used on its facade. Appropriate to its size, the entrance is in a courtyard, more deeply recessed from the street than others. The apartments have three or four rooms, those with four rooms having two bedrooms, each with a separate bath. Each unit has a dining gallery or dining alcove, but these did not count as full rooms. There are dropped living rooms. It was this building, 152 East 94th Street, which earned Boak & Paris the encomium of "famous architectural team" from an enthusiastic real estate broker in 2012.[116]

Late in 1937 they filed for a new building permit for an apartment house at 160 East 89th Street, built by Arthur Diamond, a new client for them.

---

[115] *The New York Times*, June 13, 1937, Real Estate, p. 1.

[116] *Curbed NY Marketplace*, listing updated to January 3, 2012, accessed March 9, 2012.

160 East 89th Street, between Lexington and Third Avenues, 1937-38.

It is on a fairly narrow midblock site, only nine stories in height, with the first floor designated for doctors' offices. The materials are their familiar red brick and cast stone. The facade has a center recess above its entrance, as does 50 East 78th Street – the two buildings are about the same width. The flanking windows at 50 East 78th have 90 degree corners, while those at 160 East 89th are chamfered. On its completion one year later, it was "reported fully rented."[117]

Interspersed with these taller buildings was the modest red brick, six-story nonfireproof structure at 508 West 166th Street (1937-38) for M. J. Hanover.

In sum, the years 1936 and 1937 were quite productive for Boak & Paris, and their buildings had a good deal of press notice. But following these successes came a reversal.

[117]   *The New York Times*, November 4, 1938, p. 198.

CHAPTER 5

The Riverdale Venture

Robert Moses built the Henry Hudson Bridge in record time from May 1935 to December 1936, as the linchpin in his "West Side Improvement" connecting Manhattan to Riverdale in the Bronx.[118] Seeing an opportunity to expand his real estate holdings into the Bronx, Arlington C. Hall "assembled 500,000 square feet of property"[119] and had his architects Boak & Paris draw up plans for 11 apartment houses.

While still part of Westchester County, Riverdale-on-Hudson was settled by the industrial and mercantile elite in the 1860s, when the New York Central Railroad made it possible to commute between their offices in Manhattan and their estates on "the hill." Most of the streets of Riverdale still show their origin as country lanes relating to the contours of the land rather than the grid of New York City to the south.

One section of Riverdale, Fieldston, once the estate of Joseph Delafield, was planned after the Interborough Rapid Transit brought service to 242nd Street and Broadway in 1909. Deed restrictions and covenants strictly limited development in Fieldston:

---

[118]   The full saga of the "West Side Improvement" is related in Robert Caro, *The Power Broker: Robert Moses and the Fall of New York* (New York, Vintage Books, 1975), pp. 525-66.

[119]   *The New York Times*, November 21, 1937, Real Estate, p. 1.

. . . the estate decided to develop the property by selling several acres to Manhattan Teachers College, with the rest to be a "private park devoted exclusively to country homes." The estate hired engineer Albert Wheeler, who finalized the layout in 1914. Wheeler's plan, based on recommendations made by Frederick Law Olmstead and James R. Croes, who had surveyed the area in 1876, incorporated winding roads that followed the natural topography and preserved, as far as possible, its "wooded knolls, dells and hillocks."

By 1923, the residents of the area formed the Fieldston Property Owners Association (FPOA), in order to continue the original goals of private residential development. In 1928, it published a handbook containing the names of approved architects, including, among others, Frank J. Forster, Julius Gregory, Dwight James Baum, Polhemus & Coffin, Electus D. Litchfield and James W. O'Connor. Most owners chose Baum or Gregory, . . .[120]

Fieldston streets have remained the property of the owners association, not New York City.

Just as the New York Central Railroad opened Riverdale to development and the IRT opened Fieldston, the completion of the Henry Hudson Bridge, connecting Inwood in Upper Manhattan to Riverdale, ushered in the next phase of development. This was the culmination in December 1936 of Robert Moses' goal to build a waterfront highway along the full length of Manhattan and into the Bronx, the "West Side Improvement." In anticipation that this new accessibility would result in an increase of population in Riverdale from 21,000 to 113,000, a study was made by the Mayor's Committee on City Planning (precursor to the City Planning Commission) in cooperation with the Riverdale Neighborhood Association. The study included all of the Bronx west of Broadway, with boundaries of Westchester County

[120] Landmarks Preservation Commission, City of New York, "Landmarks Preservation Commission Designates the Fieldston Historic District in the Bronx," news release, January 10, 2006.

to the north, the Harlem River to the south, and the Hudson River on the west, an area including the subcommunities known as Spuyten Duyvil, Marble Hill and Kingsbridge as well as Riverdale and Fieldston. At the time, land use was classified only as industrial, commercial and residential; Riverdale was zoned primarily residential, with much of the land vacant. The problem was how development in Riverdale would proceed without losing its character as an area of single-family homes, as a local newspaper commented at the time:

> Contrary to common belief, there is nothing in the New York City ordinance which prevents apartment houses from being built in any district. In other words, there are no single family or two family house districts, such as are commonly included in zoning ordinances elsewhere. Apartments must, of course, comply with the height and area regulations in force in the district in which they are erected.[121]

The City did not immediately act on recommendations of the report; real estate owners, including Hall, took the initiative. *The Riverdale News* for June 1937 carried a story about "New Apartment Houses, Stores, Planned Here":

> The A. C. & H. M. Hall Realty Co., of 143 West 72nd Street, who are large owners of vacant land in Riverdale, are preparing to make an application to the Board of Estimate and Apportionment to rezone from residence to business Johnson Avenue, east and west side from 100 feet north of West 235th Street to West 236th Street in Riverdale. The company contemplates the erection on the rezoned block fronts of one-story taxpayers similar in style and construction to those in Bronxville. They also propose the erection of a number of eight-story apartment houses on their adjacent and nearby properties.[122]

---

[121] "City Planning Experts Report on Riverdale Zoning," *The Riverdale News*, April 1936.

[122] *The Riverdale News*, June 1937.

On November 20, 1937 plans for 18 multi-family houses totalling
$10 million were filed with the Bronx Department of Buildings. Eleven
of these were by Boak & Paris on Hall's behalf, and the rest by other
realty companies including two companies headed by Edward L. Larkin,
architect, and Harry Colen, whose architect was G. G. Miller.

The design of these garden apartments and stores was meant to
maintain the residential character of the community:

> The general architectural scheme for the main group
> will be in early English Tudor style, with mansard roof and
> "town details blending into the beauty of the surroundings"
> according to plans drawn by Boak & Paris, architects for
> the A. C. and H. M. Hall Realty Company, which will erect
> eleven of the structures . . . The Hall group is understood to
> have assembled more than 500,000 square feet of property
> recently in the Riverdale section . . . Each apartment house
> will be of a different design. Hand-hewn half timber and
> slate will be utilized for some units and the more formal
> stone trimming of Elizabethan style in others to guard
> against monotony of design.[123]

From September to November 1937, Boak & Paris filed plans for a
total of 17 apartment and commercial buildings to be built in Riverdale
for Hall, his most ambitious project to date. They were located in the
part of lower Riverdale now cut off by the new parkway, where streets
are primarily in the rectangular grid.

Boak & Paris also filed plans in 1937 for eight eight-story apartment
houses to be built on some of the acreage of the Arrowhead Inn, on the
south side of West 246th Street west of Riverdale Avenue. These were
also to be in the English Tudor style.

The proposed development of apartment buildings was unwelcome
in the community. At a meeting of the Riverdale and Spuyten Duyvil
Property Owners Association in February 1938

---

[123]   *The New York Times*, November 21, 1937, Real Estate, p. 1.

... much opposition developed, and aside from this financial side it was pointed out that if the 5 cent subway fare was in existence in the Spuyten Duyvil and Riverdale area, this section will soon be transformed into a nesting place for ordinary apartments similar to Kingsbridge, Fordham Heights and Washington Heights which are served by the Lexington Avenue subway, the Broadway subway and the Independent subway systems.

While it was agreed by all that eventually the progress of the City would engulf the one spot in Northern New York City which remains a delightful place to live in, it would be the height of folly to hurry along the evil day, which will undoubtedly come.[124]

Anti-Semitism probably played a role, as these property owners would have been aware that the many new apartment houses in Washington Heights and Inwood were a magnet for German and Austrian Jews displaced by Hitler and second- and third-generation Jews moving up from the crowded Lower East Side.

The Fieldston Property Owners sued to stop one of Hall's projects. Boak & Paris filed plans in 1938 to build a six-story apartment house for Hall at the northeast corner of Fieldston Road and Spuyten Duyvil Parkway (now Manhattan College Parkway). When Hall had purchased the land on June 6, 1938, it was zoned as an F area, where apartments were permitted. The Fieldston Property Owners Association persuaded the new City Planning Commission to create a G area zoned for single-family homes only.

Work Stopped on New Apartment House on Spuyten Duyvil Parkway

The work on the new apartment at Fieldston Road and Spuyten Duyvil Parkway was of brief duration. Now in court, the battle will follow to see whether further construction will

---

[124]   *The Riverdale News*, February 1938.

be permitted. Fieldston residents are united and prepared to do their utmost to keep their district for one-family residents only.[125]

Hall filed a petition, and eventually a decision in his favor was handed down on July 2, 1940 as reported in *The New York Times*:

> Establishment of a residence zone in which new apartment houses are prohibited was declared to be beyond the city's existing charter powers in a decision handed down yesterday by Supreme Court Justice Aaron J. Levy. This new type of district was first created in 1938 by the City Planning Commission at the request of small home owners who said that apartment-house encroachment was ruining the value of their houses.

> Justice Levy's declaration was made in ordering Edward P. Leonard, Bronx Building Superintendent, to issue a permit to Arlington C. Hall for the construction of a Class A apartment at Spuyten Duyvil Parkway and Fieldston Road . . .

> Assistant Corporation Counsel Charles C. Weinstein, who represented the city before Justice Levy, said last night that the ruling would be appealed as soon as possible. In view of its importance it is expected to go eventually to the Court of Appeals. If necessary, the city may ask new legislation enlarging its charter powers to make such restrictions as the one assailed.[126]

The Court of Appeals reversed the decision in the City's favor on April 17, 1941, and the Fieldston homeowners prevailed. The site is now occupied by the Riverdale-Yonkers Society for Ethical Culture, built in 1967.

---

[125]   *The Riverdale News*, July 15, 1938.

[126]   *The New York Times*, July 3, 1940, p. 3.

Apparently work had been started on another site: "Arlington Hall, who built several blocks of foundations last year [1938] on Johnson Ave., at West 236th St., has resumed his operations there and work is progressing rapidly to provide stores for the area."[127]

It is striking that none of these ambitious plans succeeded. Two apartment houses Hall and Boak & Paris proposed for 231st Street and Palisade Avenue were disapproved by the Department of Buildings. Hall sold one plot of land to the St. Gabriel School and Church in 1940, which could still be consistent with plans for many apartment buildings in the neighborhood. However, instead of building on the other sites, it appears Hall bided his time while the Fieldston case went through the courts. The recession of 1937 and 1938 may also have contributed to their defeat: eventually the rest of the Hall apartment house permits announced with so much fanfare in 1937 expired by limitation in January and February of 1941. Today in place of the eight eight-story apartment houses Boak & Paris planned for the Arrowhead Inn there are only single-family homes.

A proposal by Sam Minskoff of a six-story tenement at Grant Avenue and 167th Street, far from Riverdale, was scaled back to single-story stores, which stand today. Of the many applications that Boak & Paris filed to build in the Bronx in 1937 to 1939, this appears to be the sole project completed.

Boak & Paris had two major alteration projects in Manhattan in 1937-39. One was The Dorset, at 150 West 79th Street, designed by Schwartz & Gross in 1910. Originally there were two large apartments per floor, with some duplexed, having chambers above the living and dining rooms. Boak & Paris subdivided these units to make them smaller and more marketable.[128] The total cost was estimated at $100,000. The second large alteration project was The Leonori, at 26 East 63rd Street, designed as an apartment hotel by Buchman & Fox in 1901. Originally

---

[127] *Riverdale Press*, May 5, 1939.

[128] Andrew Alpern, *New York's Fabulous Luxury Apartments* (New York: Dover Publications, 1975), pp. 66-67.

there were about ten bedrooms (each with bath) and ten parlors per floor. All bedrooms and parlors had entrances directly from the foyer halls, which were public. Doors connecting adjacent rooms would have permitted combining units. Residents were expected to eat in the building's dining room. The modernizing created six apartments per floor, adding kitchens and dining alcoves, and - as was standard in Boak & Paris apartments - a foyer for each unit. "After this alteration, only the facade remained of the original building."[129]

Hyman Paris and Russell M. Boak faced another crisis in 1937 – bankruptcy as builders. On February 28, 1937, Hyman Paris, builder, filed for bankruptcy in the Southern District, with liabilities of $103,489, assets $50. Two days later, Russell M. Boak, builder, filed in the same court, with liabilities of $114,256, assets $150. The two bankruptcies were discharged on the same day, July 21, 1937.[130] The only judgment known to have been filed against the architectural firm of "Boak & Paris, Inc." was in 1936 by the State Tax Commission for $220.90.[131] It seems that the men kept their construction work legally – and apparently wisely – separate from their architectural work.

So the year 1937 was a very mixed experience for Boak & Paris: six New Building permits filed for apartment buildings in Manhattan, plus the renovation of the Dorset, all of which were completed, contrasted with the failure of the initiatives in the Bronx, plus the bankruptcies as builders. The year 1938 was worse: while the 1937 projects were being completed, there was no new work except for the renovation of the Leonori. Fortunately, in 1939 to 1941, they were able to realize a number of buildings before the United States entered World War II.

---

[129] Christopher Gray, "The Leonori: A Building that Recounts the Multiple-Dwelling Story," originally published in *The New York Times*, February 14, 1988; reprinted in *Changing New York: The Architectural Scene* (New York: Dover Publications, 1992), p. 40.

[130] *The New York Times*, March 1 and 3 and July 22, 1937.

[131] *The New York Times*, April 28, 1936.

CHAPTER 6

World War II Approaches:
A Snapshot of the Boak & Paris Office

In early 1939, Boak & Paris filed plans for two buildings for David Zipkin. Both are modest six-story buildings in the Inwood section of northern Manhattan, at 231 Sherman Avenue and 207th Street and 251 Seaman Avenue between 215th and 218th Streets. The ornament at both includes elements seen at earlier buildings. At 231 Sherman, there is an echo in cast stone of the arcoterion done in iron over the entrance of 250 Cabrini. Above the entrance to the Seaman Avenue building is a broken pediment with an urn similar to 255 Cabrini; the door is flanked by a Greek key design. While these buildings have some of the molded brick and cast stone trim of earlier buildings, they are of tan rather than the red brick frequently used by Boak & Paris in the past.

The two buildings Boak & Paris designed for Sidney and Arthur Diamond at 170 and 177 East 77th Street (1939-41) are a departure from most of their earlier designs.

170 East 77th Street, between Lexington and Third Avenues, 1939-40.

177 East 77th Street, between Lexington and Third Avenues, 1940-41.

The brick is a light tan, and the buildings are pared down, with an almost total absence of ornamental detail on their flat facades. There are wide casement windows, now with 45-degree chamfered corners, a feature they had used on a 1931 Bronx apartment house for Minskoff and a 1937 Diamond building at 160 East 89th Street. Both buildings are the same height of 100 feet, but 170 has ten stories plus penthouse, while 177 has eleven plus penthouse, meaning lower ceilings in 177. 170 has dropped living rooms, but 177 does not. Since the plots are 125 and 99 feet wide respectively, they present themselves as horizontal buildings, with minimal terracing and setbacks at their tops.

The construction method and the speed this made possible received extensive reporting in *The New York Times*:

> Exterior brick work on the new 12-story and penthouse apartment building at 177 East Seventy-seventh Street has been completed in thirty working days "to set something of a record for this type of work," according to Sidney and Arthur Diamond, owners . . .

> Modern construction methods have helped to speed up the process of erecting this large structure. Use was made of a bolting process to eliminate the noise of steel riveting. All of the steel girders and columns have been bolted together, as the work was carried out from plans by Boak & Paris, architects.

> As the steel construction progressed from floor to floor the concrete workers poured the concrete constantly within two floors of the steel workers. When the concrete workers reached the seventh floor the bricklayers started their task, and when the brick work reached the sixth floor, work on the partitions began.

> For a while the steel men, concrete men and bricklayers were all working at the same time. As a consequence of the coordinated efforts of these mechanics and because all materials and equipment had been ordered well in advance,

the steel skeleton, concrete flooring and the laying of the brick was accomplished in the unusual time of thirty working days.[132]

The 45-degree chamfered corners became very common after the war. Similar as they are, their entrances are different. The entrance to 170 on the south side of 77th Street is set back from the street in a courtyard. On the north side of 77th Street, the entrance to 177 is almost flush with the street, although there is a slight recess on upper floors affording small balconies to some front apartments. But what really sets 177 East 77th Street apart are "Private terraces in all but six of its fifty-eight apartments [which] are proving to be a primary renting inducement" since they overlooked the landscaped gardens of the two-story Cottages that faced Third Avenue.[133] The balconies, in effect, gave everyone a terrace as if they lived in a penthouse. And certainly balconies proliferated in the postwar era, even when they had no pleasant view.

In fact, these two buildings are so austere that it is easy to mistake them for postwar buildings. In *New York 1930*, Stern et al. write that these display "explicit Modernism."[134] Why the change in 1939? Surely one of the first reasons is economic: as employment picked up, the cost of labor increased gradually relative to the cost of materials. Also the 1939 World's Fair exposed everyone, Boak & Paris included, to Modernism.

Boak & Paris did one more building for the Simon Brothers, at 20 Fifth Avenue on the southwest corner of Ninth Street (1939-40).

---

[132]   *The New York Times*, July 6, 1941.

[133]   *Real Estate Record and Guide* 145, August 3, 1940, p. 7. The Cottages with their garden were demolished, despite a year-long fight to preserve them. *The New York Times*, July 23, 1999.

[134]   *New York 1930*, p. 399.

20 Fifth Avenue, at West Ninth Street, 1939-40.

The materials are red brick and cast stone, with the crossed arrow motif used on window grilles. It has the chamfered corner windows found in the Diamond buildings, but otherwise 20 Fifth Avenue, with its setbacks and terraces, appears to be a cousin of the previous Modern Classical buildings designed for the Simon Brothers, at 5 and 100 Riverside Drive. It replaced the Berkeley Hotel, which had stood at this site for 60 years.[135]

---

[135]   *The New York Times*, June 22, 1939, p. 45.

One last project Boak & Paris designed for Arlington C. Hall is the two-story building at 37 East 50th Street (1939-41).

37 East 50th Street, between Madison and Park Avenues, 1939-41. The first Howard Johnson restaurant in New York; Howard Johnson had his New York office on the second floor.

This was the first Howard Johnson restaurant in Manhattan, with a cocktail bar and seating capacity of 250. Mr. Johnson had his New York office on the second floor.[136] It has a cast stone facade, with nicely proportioned windows. Above each side window on the second floor is a modified Greek key, with a modest anthemion above it. Hardly the familiar orange roof and Colonial cupola of most Howard Johnsons!

After 1941, there are no new Boak & Paris buildings for Hall. The applications to build in Riverdale expired in January and February 1941, and Hall lost the suit to build in Fieldston in April of 1941. Hall gave his later alteration work to other architects. His collaboration with Boak & Paris had lasted more than ten years.

In 1940 Boak & Paris started working with David Rose (1890-1986), a builder whose first buildings were in the Bronx. He had "tiptoed into Manhattan" with Tryon Gardens (1936, Sugarman & Berger) and Park Terrace Gardens (1938, Albert Goldhammer), both in Northern Manhattan. "The first job Boak & Paris did for us was on 57th Street – that brought us downtown," according to Elihu Rose, Dave's nephew.[137]

Rose acquired the property in a run-down area from the Seamens Bank for Savings. The Westmore of 1940 is actually two buildings fronting on 333 West 57th Street (163 feet) and 340 West 58th Street (138 feet).

---

[136] *The New York Times*, February 8, 1941, p. 28. The Gloucester House and now Maloney & Porcelli are restaurants that have succeeded Howard Johnson's.

[137] Elihu Rose, interview by Andrew S. Dolkart, June 19, 2012, Avery Architectural & Fine Arts Library, Columbia University.

The Westmore, 333 West 57th Street,
between Eighth and Ninth Avenues, 1940.

A feature of the structure is a large garden court the width of a city street between the two units of the building. An arcade extends across the court and connects the two units. The walls of the arcade are composed of glass brick[138]

---

[138] A photo of the glass brick arcade was featured in an advertisement for Pittsburgh Corning Glass in *Architectural Record*, September 1941, p. 11.

and large panes of glass extend from the ceiling to the terrazzo floor. Glass doors lead onto flagstone garden walks. The garden court and the arcade have been excellent renting assets, according to the management.[139]

The buildings are eight stories in height, with stores on the ground floor of the 57th Street building. Both have flat roofs, with a tower masking the water tank and elevator, but no penthouse tower. There are aluminum marquees over the entrances. A light tan brick is used, and the ornament is spare, but not the radically flat facade of the Diamond buildings: each Westmore building has four projecting bays of windows, with almost continuous strip windows. Altogether, these are horizontal buildings. The dropped living room has only one step down, not two as in earlier buildings. The foyers are aligned with the living rooms, and the dining galleries are aligned with the kitchens, which usually have a window. Most apartments have one bedroom, but some have only living room, kitchen and dining gallery.

The Westmore invites comparison to the Rockefeller Apartments of Harrison & Fouilhoux (1935-36) on 54th and 55th Streets between Fifth and Sixth Avenues: small apartments that could serve as pieds-a-terre; a through-the-block courtyard; more width than height; and projecting bays, although those at the Rockefeller Apartments are semi-circular rather than angular. Boak and Paris would have been very aware of the Rockefeller Apartments since their building at 50 East 78th Street had been featured in the press in 1936 and 1937 along with the Rockefeller Apartments (see Chapter 4). Also featured in this *Real Estate Record* round-up of building for investment was 1000 Grand Concourse in which David Rose took great pride; it had been constructed in 1934 to the design by Victor Mayper, engineer, and Sugarman & Berger, architects.

Collaboration between the Rose firm and Russell Boak continued right up to the last completed Boak project. David Rose moved his

---

[139] "Brisk Market for New West Side Suites," *Real Estate Record*, January 25, 1941, p. 8.

headquarters from the Bronx to the Westmore in the 1950s. Boak lived with his wife in the Westmore from 1949 until his death in 1981.

A snapshot of the Boak & Paris office was provided by Gertrude Sklar Bell, who was recommended to Boak & Paris by Philip Birnbaum, and who worked there from 1937 until its close in 1942 at the start of World War II.[140]

The first Boak & Paris office in which Gertrude Bell worked was at 295 Madison Avenue and 41st Street in the 43rd floor penthouse with windows on all sides providing light for the drafting work.[141]

Hyman Paris was quite short, "a most unusual person, friendly, he didn't have an enemy in the world, and all his friends were tall chorus girls." Russell Boak was tall, well-dressed and good-looking -- "he looked like Gary Cooper." She said that Boak was the one in charge, although when negotiating with Minskoff, the Simon brothers and others, both Boak and Paris would be involved. Boak was the creative designer of the facades and also did floor plans and lobby designs, sometimes with an interior decorator such as Elsie de Wolfe who designed the lobby of 100 Riverside Drive.

In addition to the principals, there were Anthony Campagna, the "steel man"; about six draftsmen; and two interns. She was the only

---

[140]   Gertrude Sklar Bell, interview by the author, July 27, 2001.

[141]   It appears that all their offices were in buildings with unobstructed light. Boak & Paris' office from 1927-30, was at 11 West 42nd Street, designed by York & Sawyer, 1926, which faces the New York Public Library. From 1930-33, their office was at 10 East 40th Street, Ludlow & Peabody, 1928. Then from 1934-37 they were in the Architects Building, 101 Park Avenue at 40th Street, designed by Ewing & Chappell and LaFarge & Morris, 1912 (demolished). From 1937 to 1940, they were at 295 Madison Avenue at 41st Street, Bark & Djorup, 1928-30. Then 1940 to 1942, they were at 18 East 41st Street, designed by George and Edward Blum, 1912-14. Finally Boak & Raad from 1944-65, and Russell M. Boak Associates to 1972, had offices at the Flatiron Building, 175 Fifth Avenue at 23rd Street, Daniel Burnham, 1901-03.

woman in the office, and she had so much typing of specifications ("seven carbon copies!") that she would take work home on weekends.

Gertrude Bell said Boak loved his work and would call her over and show her what he was doing. Mr. Campagna also would show her drawings of the steel work and explain that he was designing so that buildings could sway.

She said that she had always wondered what the exact relationship was between Mr. Boak and Mr. Paris, and she believes that Mr. Paris had the license while Mr. Boak did not. Subsequent inquiry to the State Education Department in Albany showed that her hunch was right; Hyman Paris was licensed in 1922, and Russell Boak only in 1941.[142]

Some days she would come to work "dressed up like Lady Astor," and visit sites where new apartment buildings were going up. She would pretend to be interested in renting an apartment and ask for floor plans. Then she would take these back to the office. "Everyone did it," she said; "it was one of the tricks of the trade."[143] This was how Mr. Boak knew what other architects were doing; he would never just imitate them, but adapt and make the design his own, she said. They also subscribed to the leading architectural magazines, which she loved to study.

Hyman Paris was Jewish. Russell Boak was not; she thinks he may have been Episcopalian. Mrs. Bell always took the Jewish holidays, and so did Mr. Patterson, one of the draftsmen who, she believes, had changed his name. Mr. Campagna and Irving Guerasio, one of the interns, were Italian. She recognizes that this mix of Jews and Gentiles

---

[142] New York State Education Department, e-mail message to the author, July 31, 2001.

[143] Boak & Paris was not the only architectural office to collect brochures and floor plans. Robert L. Bien donated to Avery Library at Columbia University a collection of brochures and floor plans of over 250 apartment buildings and many commercial buildings from his own practice and that of his father Sylvan Bien and many other New York architects.

in the same architectural firm was unusual for the time.[144] Similarly, some of their major clients such as Samuel Minskoff, Jacob and Arthur Simon and David Rose, were Jewish, while others like William J. Hanna and Arlington C. Hall were not.

As the War approached and material was diverted to armaments, architectural work dried up and the part-time draftsmen were let go, one by one. When the firm moved to a smaller office at 18 East 41ˢᵗ Street in late 1940, only she, Campagna, and the two interns were still with Boak and Paris. The United States had already entered World War II when she left in early 1942 to work for the War Manpower Commission.

The firm had some alteration jobs. In June 1942, "Modernization work costing $35,000 has been completed in the six-story building at 73 Warren Street, which was purchased recently by the Edwards Employment Agencies . . . from plans by Boak & Paris, architects, and Joseph Lau, associate architect."[145] Apparently these alterations were only interior. This 1880 building by John Hoffman, architect, is in Romanesque Revival style, with a fine red terra cotta facade. The cornice was removed after 1940. Otherwise, the original facade appears to be intact, including a ground floor with limestone surrounding segmentally arched windows and an arch the full width of the building at the fifth floor.

Boak stated that he practiced alone from 1942 to 1944,[146] and his name alone is on an alteration application filed in April of 1942, "rearranging partitions on 5ᵗʰ flr to create 2 apts from one" at 190

---

[144] "It is notable that many of the architects specializing in apartment house design were Jewish, marking the first generation of Jews to enter the American architectural profession in large numbers. Many of the clients were also Jews, reflecting the emergence of established Jewish New Yorkers as a major force in the local building and real estate communities." Andrew S. Dolkart and Susan Tunick, *George and Edgar Blum: Texture and Design in New York Apartment House Architecture* (New York: Friends of Terra Cotta Press, 1993), footnote 16.

[145] *The New York Times*, June 15, 1942, p. 31.

[146] Boak, AIA application.

Riverside Drive. The White Plains directory for 1942 lists Mabel Boak, beauty operator at B. Altman & Co., living at 23 Old Mamaroneck Road, and R. M. Boak also residing there, but lists no occupation for him.[147]

Boak & Paris stayed three years in each of its previous offices, so Boak might have stayed at 18 East 41st Street through 1943, although there is no listing in the 1943 New York Telephone Directory for either Russell Boak or Hyman Paris.

Emery Roth's biography says that while his sons were away during the War, Roth

> did not allow himself to be totally alone [at 18 East 48th Street]. Because his office was virtually devoid of human activity other than his own, he made an offer to several other architects that they share his space rent-free. Since they had a limited amount of work at that time, he generously provided a convenient working arrangement whereby his colleagues could keep each other company and still be able to prepare their drawings at minimal expense.[148]

These architects are not named, so it is not possible to know whether Boak or Paris benefitted from Roth's generosity.[149]

While Boak may have spent some of the War in Roth's office, there is one clue concerning what he worked on during the War. Elihu Rose, who knew Boak in the 1950s and 1960s, states that

> I distinctly remember Russ telling me that he was working on an unspecified project that, unbeknownst to him at the time, had something to do with development of

---

147   *Polk's White Plains (Westchester County, N.Y.) City Directory, 1942.* (Boston, MA: R. L. Polk & Co., 1942).

148   *Mansions in the Clouds*, p. 185.

149   It appears that Hyman Paris died in 1966; Social Security Death Index.

the atomic bomb. What the mysterious project was, I have no idea.[150]

The three main sites of the Manhattan Project, as the development of the atomic bomb was called, were Oak Ridge, Tennessee, Los Alamos, New Mexico and Hanford, Washington. Of these, Oak Ridge was by far the largest. For Oak Ridge, John O. Merrill of Skidmore, Owings & Merrill was in charge of a team that ultimately numbered 180. At its peak, the Manhattan Project had more than 200,000 workers at 37 installations.[151] So it is still mysterious exactly where Boak worked and what he did in World War II.

---

[150]   Elihu Rose, personal letter to author, March 15, 2013.

[151]   Charles W. Johnson and Charles O. Jackson, *City Behind a Fence: Oak Ridge, Tennessee, 1942-1946* (Knoxville, University of Tennessee Press, 1981), pp. 14-15 ff. Also Joel Davidson, "Building for War, Preparing for Peace," in *World War II and the American Dream: How Wartime Building Changed a Nation*, Donald Albrecht, ed. (Cambridge, The MIT Press, 1994), p. 213.

CHAPTER 7

Boak & Raad Postwar: The Doelger Block

World War II ended in August 1945, with an enormous pent-up demand for housing. Price and rent controls were kept in place for some time and significantly delayed the start of what became a postwar construction boom.[152]

Russell Boak formed a new partnership in 1944 with Thomas O. Raad, like him born in New York City in 1896. Raad's prior career had much less continuity than Boak's. He attended the College of the City of New York and Columbia University for one year each. Like Boak, he started working while still a student in high school, and was successively office boy, junior and then senior draftsman in several firms. He served in the U.S. Navy in 1917-18. From 1921 to 1935, he was squad boss or senior draftsman at Seelig & Finkelstein, Schwartz & Gross, Chanin Construction Co. and the City Department of Parks. He and Edward W. Franklin were partners in architectural practice from 1936 to 1943. Raad became licensed in New York in 1930, in New Jersey in 1943,

---

[152] "Why the Lag in Housing Construction?" *Real Estate Forum*, September 1946, pp. 10-11, and "Vast Housing Plans Await 'Free' Market," *Real Estate Forum*, February 1947, pp. 12 ff.

and in Pennsylvania in 1955.[153] Boak and Raad remained partners until Raad's retirement in 1965.

Boak & Raad filed New Building applications while the war was still on. On July 24, 1944, they filed plans for a 19-story apartment building on Sixth Avenue, 56th to 57th Street; their building for Andros Realty was finally built in 1960, with a different appearance.[154] Two days later, they filed plans for the Diamonds for a ten-story apartment house at 211-21 East 78th Street, which was not built. Nor was their proposal on behalf of Emigrant Savings Bank for a 15-story building at Madison and 89th Street. In 1945 Simon Brothers planned a tall building for Fifth Avenue and 68th Street, naming Russell M. Boak as architect[155]; instead the design was done in 1946 by William I. Hohauser.

It appears that the first completed Boak & Raad building was for David Rose, and the collaboration with David Rose or Rose Associates continued for the rest of Boak's career. The 15-story Thornley (1945-46) at 215 East 79th Street has many similarities to the Westmore of 1940: light brick, almost no ornamentation on the facade, flat roof, aluminum marquees, and the same relatively spacious dimension of rooms.

---

[153] Thomas O. Raad Application for corporate membership in the American Institute of Architects No. 12871, granted September 6, 1957, AIA Archives, Washington, DC. He and Boak submitted their applications on the same date and were approved at the same time.

[154] See below, Chapter 9.

[155] *The New York Times*, May 18, 1945.

The Thornley, 215 East 79th Street,
between Third and Second Avenues, 1945-46.

Both have sunken living rooms and triple-width bay casement windows. While the Westmore at eight stories is horizontal, the Thornley at 15 stories appears more vertical, topped by setbacks and balconies. Typically six units per floor, the suites were 2-1/2 to 4-1/2 rooms, with one or two bedrooms. Its very symmetrical facade recalls prewar designs. However, unlike prewar apartments, the building is fully air-conditioned with individual room controls.

As World War II was coming to an end, on the front page of the Real Estate section of *The New York Times* for Sunday, June 10, 1945 was the announcement of plans to build seven apartment buildings on the Doelger Brewery block, Sutton Place to First Avenue, 55th to 56th Streets -- a project long in gestation and long in construction. The brewer Peter Doelger had started acquiring land "uptown" in 1856 when it was open country, and established his family in a brownstone residence next to the brewery, completing acquisition of this block by 1900. According to *The New York Times*,

> The section developed into a tenement area, but about 1915 began to turn into a choice residential neighborhood when some of the Morgan and Vanderbilt families pioneered by moving there. It was not long before large apartment buildings began to line Fifty-seventh Street from Second Avenue to the East River, and it became evident that the site had outgrown its use for brewery purposes. Values rose appreciably, and in 1929 the entire brewery block was sold to the Chanins for $5,500,000. A few years later the Doelgers reacquired the block through the Delagart Corporation.[156]

William E. P. Doelger (1901-1992), grandson of the founder and then head of the family business, conceived a plan in 1939 to build an apartment complex on the block.[157] The initial Boak & Raad plan announced in 1945 proposed two 19-story buildings on Sutton Place

---

[156] *The New York Times*, January 5, 1947, Real Estate, p 1.

[157] *The New York Times*, September 21, 1952, Real Estate, p. 1; no architect is identified for the 1939 scheme.

South anchoring the corners of 55th Street and 56th Streets, balanced by a single blockfront building facing First Avenue. Between them were to be four buildings, eight and twelve stories, the south buildings shorter in order not to block the sunlight. They would stand apart from one another, separated by broad courts. These four buildings were unusual: their shape was not dictated by the lot line, but are double cruciform shape to provide more light and air to each apartment, and are set at an angle to the street.[158] These four resemble the cruciform towers of Castle Village (1938-39), designed by George Fred Pelham II.

A new monthly magazine, the *Real Estate Forum*, started appearing in 1946, for which the Real Estate Board of New York would supply editorial material and a subscription was included in the membership dues for all REBNY member firms.[159] Early on, it became the practice to feature a new building in each issue, with background information on the owner, the architect, and every contractor, subcontractor and supplier involved in the building. The contractors and suppliers, in turn, took out ads in the *Real Estate Forum*. Often there were photographs of the principals, the owner and the architect, as well as of the building.

The first of the Doelger buildings to rise and to get this coverage in the *Real Estate Forum* was 36 Sutton Place South at 55th Street.[160] The subtitle summarizes the project: "Cornerstone of a Unique Redevelopment Project; Subsidiary of Peter Doelger Transforming Sutton Place 'Brewery Block' into Luxury Residential Neighborhood. Individual Design for Each Building Will Avoid 'Institutional' Appearance for $15,000,000 Group."

In the article it is reported that

> Rapidly rising construction costs which ran the estimated price of the building from $1,400,000 in 1945 to $2,600,000

---

[158]   *The New York Times*, June 10, 1945, Real Estate, p. 1.

[159]   *Real Estate Forum*, Vol I, #1, February 1946, p. 22.

[160]   Contrary to the normal pattern in Manhattan, on Sutton Place South numbers run from north to south.

in 1948, resulted in the redesigning of the structure, entailing many simplifications of plan and elimination of duplex apartments [which] reduced the estimated construction costs to approximately $1,800,000.[161]

The height was lowered from 19 to 17 stories. In addition, to save time, construction was changed from structural steel to reinforced concrete: "The structure is unique in that it represents one of, if not the first tall multiple dwelling constructed in New York City the frame of which is entirely of reinforced concrete" -- previously reinforced concrete would be used only to a given height and the top finished with structural steel.[162]

> The frank approach to exterior design through disregard for symmetry and with emphasis on proper fenestration for the rooms has resulted in facades of unusual informal interest. A strong accent on both the Sutton Place and 55th Street facades formed by the projecting balconies with glass and iron railings and extending from the third to the sixteenth floors, relieves the plainness of the unsymmetrical facades and lends a definite modern touch to the building.

> A colonial brick of variegated shades of warm tones of red has been used for front and rear facades of the building . . . Indiana limestone in simple horizontal treatment has been used for the lower portion of the building . . . The owners' and architects' objective has been realized in the desire to create a residential building, with diversified well-planned apartments, exterior of smart simplicity, and *a structure that will not be "dated" through any natural change in style trends in design or planning.*[163]

This mattered because this was to be the first of eight buildings planned for the block, and they didn't want it to set the design pattern.

---

[161] "36 Sutton Place South: Cornerstone of a Unique Redevelopment Project," *Real Estate Forum*, June 1949, p. 26.

[162] *Real Estate Forum*, June 1949, p. 27.

[163] *Real Estate Forum*, June 1949, pp. 27-28, emphasis added.

Yet 36 Sutton Place South had the prewar feature of steel casement windows at the building corners and at the recesses for the balconies. It also had the postwar feature of large glass picture windows.

The floor arrangement gave two or more exposures for most apartments, and an East River or garden view for all. Apartments range from two to five rooms, with two penthouse apartments of six and a half rooms. Apartments have one, two and a few three bedrooms. Foyers and living rooms continue to be aligned, as are the dining bays and kitchens, but in reversed position: the dining bays are on outer walls with windows, while kitchens are interior without windows. Other luxury features included electrical wiring sufficient to permit future installation of a ton or more of air conditioning and a master television antenna.[164]

The next Doelger buildings to go up were the "angular saw-tooth-plan" apartment buildings at 440 and 430 East 56th Street, completed in 1950 and 1952.[165] "All windows will be corner windows . . . made possible by an irregular facade designed to give additional light and air and broader views of the East River."[166] The living rooms are not dropped, but a few apartments have dining balconies, up a step. "The buildings are surrounded by garden plots; the rear gardens, which could have been concealed from view, are left visible from the street, a sensitive touch."[167] There is also a tennis club, with entry through 430 East 56th Street.

---

[164] 36 Sutton Place South was the setting for the 1953 movie "How to Marry a Millionaire," where "the bachelorette pad is the very vision of New York as a 'high and mighty, bright and shiny, fabulous place' as the song goes [worth] $10 million to $12 million" in 2011. Justin Davidson, "The Apartment: A History of Vertical Living," *New York*, April 11, 2011, p. 57.

[165] "440 East 56th Street," *Real Estate Forum*, October 1950, pp. 20-25; "430 East 56th Street," *Real Estate Forum*, September 1952, pp. 20-27. Boak & Raad is identified as "the same firm" who designed, among other buildings, 5 Riverside Drive, 100 Riverside Drive and 20 Fifth Avenue, all of them designs by the prewar Boak & Paris; *Forum*, October 1950, p. 20.

[166] *The New York Times*, January 29, 1950, Real Estate p. 1.

[167] Christopher Gray, "2 Little-Known Architects of Distinctive Buildings," Streetscapes, *The New York Times*, July 15, 2001, Real Estate, p. 7.

Although an area almost equal to one-fourth of the block will be utilized for the garage and tennis club project, and the improvement itself will not pay any return commensurate with the value of the land, Mr. Doelger explained that it would be worth while because it would create a desirable environment for the adjoining apartment houses.[168]

The last of Boak & Raad's buildings on the Doelger block, built in 1952-55, is 20 Sutton Place South at 56th Street.

20 Sutton Place South, and East 56th Street, 1952-55.

---

[168]   *The New York Times*, September 21, 1952, Real Estate, p. 1.

The first three of these Doelger buildings were rentals, but 20 Sutton Place South was planned as a luxury cooperative, which may explain why Rosario Candela and Paul Resnick participated as associate architects in its design.[169]

> In this new cooperative, the sponsors and architects have attempted to create something of the space luxury of buildings built in the 1920's. There will be pantries and large entrance foyers, features which are not customarily included in today's construction.[170]

In place of dining bays, the apartments have full dining rooms. Its unadorned Sutton Place facade is varied with recessed and forward planes, permitting chamfered windows. Twenty is taller than 36, and floors are not aligned in the two buildings because reinforced concrete construction of 20 had a thinner floor slab, "saving about 6" per floor for the same unobstructed ceiling height."[171]

The prices for these luxury cooperatives in 1954 ranged from as little as "$2850 for a one room bath and terrace apartment . . . up to $40,850 for the 9 room, 5 bath and terrace (with wood burning fireplace) penthouse apartment." Annual maintenance charges would be about 20 percent of the sales price.[172]

Across 55th Street from the Doelger block, "with extra-wide studio windows overlook[ing] the courts of the exclusive Tennis Club, . . . 412 East 55th Street is the fifth beautiful and spacious apartment building erected since 1949 by Peter Doelger, Inc. on land held and accumulated by the Doelger family for a century."[173]

---

[169]   *The New York Times*, October 25, 1953, Real Estate, p. 1.

[170]   *Real Estate Forum*, September 1954, p. 18.

[171]   *Ibid.*, p. 18.

[172]   *Ibid.*, pp. 25-26.

[173]   "412 East 55th Street," *Real Estate Forum*, December 1955, pp. 46-53.

The architects in every instance have been Boak and
Raad, who have achieved notable variety while displaying
throughout, their characteristic flair for spacious interior
layouts with truly magnificent closet and window space.[174]

This rental building turned out to be the last Boak & Raad building
for Doelger:

> Though two other apartment buildings are scheduled for
> completion in 1956 by the Doelgers, there is a possibility that
> they may mark the company's last investment in residential
> construction on Manhattan for a few years to come. Recalling
> that real estate booms do not necessarily go on forever and
> may even reach a point of diminishing returns, William
> Doelger seems to feel that the immediate future calls for
> caution, in view of the intensive residential construction
> throughout the metropolitan area in recent years.[175]

The two Boak & Raad buildings that William Doelger had planned
for the north side of 55th Street were not built, the site being partially
occupied by an enlarged garage, incorporating parts of the old brewery
walls. Nor was the 19-story design they proposed for First Avenue
built[176]; instead there is a 38-story building of 1966 by Philip Birnbaum.
All of these changes deprive us of the opportunity to experience the full
effect of Boak & Raad's planned ensemble.[177]

---

[174] *Real Estate Forum*, December 1955, p. 48.

[175] *Real Estate Forum*, December 1955, p. 53.

[176] Boak & Raad filed New Building applications in 1961 to complete their original
design; by that time, the Doelger interests had sold the property to new owners
who did not use Boak & Raad.

[177] "New Construction Has Not Destroyed Charm of Sutton Place," according to
an article in *Real Estate Record and Builders Guide*, July 29, 1961, p. 2. Sutton
Place-Sutton Place South, 53rd to 59th Streets, has eight new and six prewar luxury
apartment houses, with Robert L. Bien's 35 Sutton Place just open for occupancy
appropriating "the last available plot with frontage on the river . . . [N]one of
Sutton's famed town houses has felt the wrecker's bar."

CHAPTER 8

The Principal Clients:
Minskoff & Sons, Rose Associates

Even as the Doelger "brewery block" was being transformed into a country-club atmosphere, Boak & Raad continued to work with longtime client Sam Minksoff. Sam Minskoff & Sons commissioned Boak & Raad to design Halsey House, at 63-33 98th Place, from 63rd Road to 63rd Drive, adjoining Forest Hills, in Queens, built in 1947-49.

Halsey House, 98th Place and 63rd Road, Rego Park, Queens, 1947-49.

One can see it as transitional between prewar and postwar styles: while its eight stories are clad in the red brick and cast stone Boak & Paris used so often in their 1930s buildings, the classical ornamentation is simpler and flatter. Where many of their prewar buildings had corner windows, Halsey House has corner balconies. The balcony floors project from the building's plane and are of white cast stone, not brick, so they are very prominent. Prewar the balconies of 177 East 77th Street on the back corner of the building are relatively private, their placement determined by the view to the landscaped garden; at Halsey House, the balconies are at the street corners, the most public placement possible.

The Gramercy House (first called Park Gramercy House) for David Rose and Associates at 7 Lexington Avenue and 22nd Street (1949-51) is on the site of the home of Peter Cooper, the founder of Cooper Union.[178]

The Rose group bought the land from the Russell Sage Foundation, which had once planned a library there. The *Real Estate Forum* of August 1950 says that

> . . . the firm of David Rose & Associates is among the outstanding builders in the Metropolitan New York area and has held a pre-eminent position for over two decades. Altogether the group has built for its own ownership and management over 5000 apartments in Metropolitan New York. The company never builds for speculation and continues to own and operate every structure which it puts up.[179]

An early rendering for "Gramercy Park June 30, 1948 David E. Rose Bldg, Boak & Raad archts" has a more complex design.

---

[178]   *The New York Times*, April 16, 1950, Real Estate, p. 1.

[179]   "The Park Gramercy," *Real Estate Forum*, August 1950, pp. 18-22.

Gramercy House, 7 Lexington Avenue, and East 22nd Street, 1949-51.

Gramercy House, 7 Lexington Avenue, 1948 design.

Its silhouette would have harkened back to Boak's 1930s buildings: at 15 stories it would have been taller with more setbacks and terraces, and darker brick for spandrels. As built, it is 12 stories with a flat roof except for an elevator tower, and a simple cornice with a metal railing. The facade is of light cream brick with no adornment except its windows. The rental brochure says it features picture windows[180] and corner windows for cross ventilation -- but also outlets for installing air conditioners under the bedroom and living room windows. The "beautiful decor in the main lobby is being designed by Mr. Boak of the architectural firm." The apartments are only two to three-and-a-half rooms, but

> there is an outside kitchen and distinct dining bay or dining balcony for each apartment. This is a definite departure from current trends toward interior kitchens and combination living and dining rooms . . . The Rose organization reasons that the small family finds it just as important to have adequate dining space as a larger family and that there is no reason for penalizing the small family just because it happens to be small.[181]

Boak & Raad designed 20 East 68th Street at Madison Avenue (1954-56) for Rose. Unlike other Rose buildings, this building does not have a name; its good address is enough to distinguish it. Here the living and dining rooms are combined but spacious: "Living-dining areas will be available up to thirty-five feet in length and bedrooms will be as long as nineteen and one-half feet . . . Designs of granite and marble will be used in the lobby and entranceway. This decorative scheme will be continued on the outside, where a facade of granite will extend around

---

[180]   The picture window is what is known as a "*Chicago window*. A window occupying the full width of a bay and divided into a large fixed sash flanked by a narrow movable sash on each side, as in the Marquette building by HOLABIRD & ROCHE (1894) and SULLIVAN's Carson Pirie & Scott store (1899-1904) in Chicago." *The Penguin Dictionary of Architecture*, by John Fleming, Hugh Honour and Nikolaus Pevsner. London and New York: Penguin Books, 1991, p. 91.

[181]   "The Park Gramercy," *Real Estate Forum*, August 1950, pp. 18-22.

the building up to the second floor. The glazed brickwork of the upper stories will be a pearl gray color."[182]

This building introduced a new concept in air conditioners:

> Dave [Rose] thought inelegant the window air conditioners that stuck out into the street and dripped on passersby, but no other kinds of units were available. He eventually found a manufacturer that would listen, and proposed they jointly design a unit no thicker than the wall of an apartment house, no higher than from floor to window, and able to exhaust through a grill or grate flush with the outside line of the building. He offered to pay all development and manufacturing costs for machining enough such units for two of his buildings currently under construction, with the proviso that if the "under-window" units became popular and an assembly line was begun to produce them, Dave would have the privilege of retroactively paying the lowest production price available. That's how Chrysler's under-window air conditioners became a standard feature of postwar apartment houses.[183]

The function of windows now changed from ventilation and light combined to providing light alone. The window strips could be three even five across, sometimes with a fixed center window. If more heat came in through such an expanse of glass, cooling could be achieved through air conditioners. Apartment layouts no longer needed to provide cross ventilation. The little setbacks and recesses that had permitted corner casement windows in prewar buildings were no longer necessary. The skin of the building could be flatter - a trend Boak & Raad did not always follow.

---

[182] *The New York Times*, November 14, 1954, Real Estate p. 1.

[183] Tom Shachtman, *Skyscraper Dreams: The Great Real Estate Dynasties of New York* (Boston: Little, Brown and Company, 1991), p. 206.

Boak & Raad were commissioned to design two large apartment buildings on Sailors Snug Harbor land in Greenwich Village. In 1801 the Revolutionary War privateer Robert Richard Randall had required his trustees to set up a home for "aged decrepit and worn-out sailors" and deeded 12 acres of his farm for the purpose. But land in Greenwich Village was too valuable to be devoted to such a retirement home, so Sailors Snug Harbor was built on Staten Island, while the Village land was leased to provide an income stream. In the 1950s, most of this land was redeveloped with large apartment buildings.[184] David Rose is quoted in the *Real Estate Forum*:

> A section that only a few years back housed decaying loft buildings and antique residences converted to business or rooming-house use, has today become the scene of a $50,000,000 residential building boom, with some 4000 new apartment units contemplated, under way or completed. No other part of the city has seen such a high concentration of quality residential building and building-plans in so short a time.[185]

Randall House is a block-long building on Broadway at 63 East Ninth Street, extending to Tenth Street (1954-55).

---

[184]   Robert A. M. Stern, Thomas Mellins, and David Fishman, *New York 1960: Architecture and Urbanism Between the Second World War and the Bicentennial* (New York: The Monacelli Press, 1995), pp. 222-23.

[185]   "Randall House: 63 East 9th Street," *Real Estate Forum*, November 1955, pp. 28-40.

Randall House, 63 East Ninth Street, and Broadway, 1954-55.

The red brick facades on Broadway and Ninth Street rise straight up from the lot line to the 12th story, with duplex penthouses above set well back so that they are barely visible from the street. On Ninth Street there is a section west of the entrance which rises only six stories, probably because of zoning on side streets. Randall House has stores on Broadway and an underground garage – in fact, underground garages were standard in their buildings from this time on. The building is U-shaped, with a substantial interior courtyard. "Boak and Raad have made effective use of the popular L-shaped and double-L layouts, which provide a pleasing change from old-style cubicle room design and effectively separate living from dining and foyer areas without breaking up the overall floor-space." The 230 ultra-modern apartments are two to four and a half rooms, with "12 duplex penthouses each with its own studio and roof garden, in an unusual utilization of rooftop space pioneered by Mr. Rose."[186]

Another innovation at Randall House was an exhibit called Decorama "originated by David Rose and prepared by Beryl S. Austrian and Carl Norris of Intramural, Inc . . . Rather than presenting one or two model furnished apartments in the conventional manner, which is designed more to merchandise new furniture than to assist tenants in placing their own cherished pieces in a new apartment, Decorama presents some 50 watercolor sketches illustrating the various uses of the rooms themselves [complete with] samples of wall paint and swatches of harmonizing floor covering, upholstery an drapery fabrics."[187]

The second project on Sailors Snug Harbor land is The Brevoort, which Sam Minksoff & Sons built in 1954-55 to Boak & Raad design. It replaced several town houses including one once occupied by Mark Twain and the well-loved (but vacant) Brevoort Hotel.[188]

---

[186] *Ibid.*, p. 29.

[187] *Ibid.*, p. 38.

[188] "The Brevoort: Proud Heir to an Illustrious Name," *Real Estate Forum*, July 1955, pp. 24-33.

The Brevoort, 11 Fifth Avenue, East Eight to Ninth Streets, 1954-56.

The Brevoort seems to have been influenced by the first "white brick" apartment building, Manhattan House, at 200 East 66th Street, designed by Skidmore, Owings & Merrill and Mayer & Whittlesey for New York Life Insurance Co., completed in 1950. The Brevoort is clad in a buff brick. Closer to hand and more related in layout is Two Fifth Avenue designed in 1950 by Richard Roth of Emery Roth & Sons for the Rudin interests.

The Brevoort, like Randall House, occupies a full blockfront at 11 Fifth Avenue from Eighth to Ninth Streets. However, the massing of the two is different: Randall House rises to its full height of 12 stories almost without setbacks, while the Brevoort has low-rise wings on the side streets and five setback penthouse floors above the core, 14 stories in all. The entrance to the Brevoort is recessed from Fifth Avenue, with a porte cochere. So while Randall House is a very horizontal block, the Brevoort has some of the symmetry and setbacks of prewar Boak & Paris buildings. The postwar Boak & Raad of the Brevoort is in contrast to the prewar Boak & Paris' 20 Fifth Avenue facing it: the ornamentation is gone, as well as the slender tapering.

The Brevoort had air-conditioning units in all living rooms and bedrooms, but also cross ventilation:

> The H-shaped design, together with the great number of facade indentations and setbacks, will permit maximum cross and through ventilation. In addition, apartments from the second through the 14th floors along the Fifth Avenue frontage will feature open, corner balconies as an additional note of luxury.[189]

Some residents have since enclosed these cantilevered balconies, thus recreating the corner window.

Boak & Raad as associate architects contributed to the design of the lobby of the Eastmore. This was the second Rose building along with the contemporaneous 20 East 68th Street to have under-window air conditioners. Leo Stillman, who designed more than 50 buildings for the Rose organization, was the lead architect for this 17-story apartment house at 240 East 76th Street extending on Second Avenue to 75th Street (1954-56).[190] It is another very horizontal block similar to Randall House. The Eastmore had the smallest rooms that the Rose firm ever

---

[189]   *Ibid.*, p. 28.

[190]   "Eastmore House: David Rose's New Apartments Offer Many Innovations," *Real Estate Forum*, November 1956, pp. 35-47.

built, and probably because of that, according to Elihu Rose, it "was a money printing house from the first day. It mortgaged out – it was built for less than the mortgage. The Eastmore had a marvelous reputation with young people coming to New York. You come to New York, you stay at the Barbizon until you get an apartment in Eastmore House."[191]

Russell Boak and Thomas Raad became certified architects in Pennsylvania in 1955, and did an apartment house at 220 West Rittenhouse Square at Locust Street, Philadelphia, for E. J. Frankel in 1956. The site had been occupied by a venerable library, and in the new building the branch of the Philadelphia Free Library occupies the ground floor on the side street, while the apartment lobby faces Rittenhouse Square. The ground floor is of cast stone, with the shaft of tan brick rising 24 stories. The facade is flat, marked by three strips of windows to the 14th floor; then at the 15th, the outer two strips are replaced by recessed balconies.

In 1957, Boak and Raad, both then 61, applied and were accepted for membership in the American Institute of Architects, the nation's leading organization for the architectural profession. While it is not unusual for architects to join late in their careers, both of them would have been eligible to apply years earlier. Since 1943 they had belonged to the New York Society of Architects, the organization primarily of members of small firms. Did they delay applying to the AIA because they felt that the AIA would not be welcoming to those without academic degrees in architecture? The year 1957 was the centennial for the AIA, which may have then been soliciting new members. But perhaps it was that in 1955-56 Boak & Raad lost out on four projects on the East Side of Manhattan for which they had filed new building applications,[192] so it may have seemed desirable to be able to add "AIA" to their signatures.

---

[191] Elihu Rose, interview by Andrew S. Dolkart, June 20, 2012, Avery Architectural & Fine Arts Library, Columbia University.

[192] The unsuccessful applications were for 510 East 86th Street, 955 Madison Avenue, 475 Park Avenue, and 243 East 68th Street.

CHAPTER 9

Diversifying the Client Base

Postwar, and especially in the 1950s and 1960s, buildings tended to be bigger than prewar -- blockfronts or even full blocks. The total number of Boak & Raad projects was fewer than the Boak & Paris output, but each was larger and took longer to construct. The era was very competitive; new projects might be filed, but the property might be sold to a new developer who then built with a different architect. So while in the 1930s *all* of the new building applications Boak & Paris filed in Manhattan were actually built, postwar a number of the Boak & Raad new building applications were built years later or never built.

The demolition of the Third Avenue El in 1955 precipitated a building boom, including a building on the prominent intersection of 72nd Street and Third Avenue. Boak & Raad filed a New Building permit in 1956 for 165 East 72nd Street extending to 73rd Street.

James J. Secoles was owner as well as builder of this apartment house on Manhattan's "New Third Avenue." On its corner stone is engraved "ERECTED 1959/J. J. SECOLES BUILDER/BOAK & RAAD ARCHITECTS." In 1933, J. J. Secoles, Inc. had been the builder of the Midtown Theater for Arlington C. Hall.

165 East 72nd Street, and Third Avenue, 1956-59.

The brochure for the new building claims that "The architectural style of the building as well as the interior design of the lobby and halls will be in keeping with the modern Colonial character followed by other buildings in the immediate area and will be executed in dignified and conservative taste."[193] The building is clad in red brick, but the most "Colonial" element seems to be the bank (originally First National City Bank, now Citibank), with its Georgian large eight-over-eight windows, while the apartment windows above are generic 1950s sash windows, in groups of two, three and five. It has setbacks and terraces that rise to two stubby towers, more like Central Park West of the 1930s than Colonial.

It houses stores on its Second Avenue front, and rises 20 stories over the avenue, with units ranging from two to six rooms, including some three-bedrooms. Dining and living rooms form an L up to 23 feet in width. This was one of six luxury skyscraper buildings on 72nd Street, from Fifth to First Avenue under construction in 1958, with rents at or above $100/room/month.[194]

Westminster House is the corner building at 55 East 85th Street at Madison, linked by a small garden to a narrow building through the block at 52 East 86th Street (1957-58). There are stores on the ground floor of the Madison Avenue front. The owner was Stanley Broff, whose father Irving had built the prewar 5 West 86th Street of Boak & Paris. With this new building, Stanley fulfilled a wish of his father to buy this site, the location of the original P.S. 6.[195]

> [The 85th Street building] spreads over 14 floors with horizontal ease, recessed and indented for an esthetic variation of design that functionally allowed an abundant extravagance of L-shaped walls of glass . . . Its companion, fronting on 86th Street, points skyward in a commanding verticality of line achieved without sacrificing in any way the broad expanse of picture windows that are found in almost

---

[193]   Brochure in collection of Andrew Alpern.

[194]   *The New York Times*, October 5, 1958, p. 1.

[195]   "35 East 85th Street: Stanley Broff's New Project Combines Elegance with Exacting Standards of Modern Construction," *Real Estate Forum*, July 1958, pp. 56-67.

every room of the two structures. Together the buildings complement each other in a rare architectural harmony.[196]

The feature article in the *Real Estate Forum* continues,

> Surmounted on the marble-and-granite base is a shining sweep of white glazed enamel brick accented with black spattering that soars to the top towers. No court brick is used anywhere; the face brick appears everywhere over the entire exterior so that " . . . no matter where you look," notes Mr. Broff, "you see a 'building front'." . . .

> The bricklaying method also commands attention. Instead of the 50 or 60 "boots" usually employed for a project of this size, Mr. Broff is using only 20 men -- each a handpicked master mason, specially skilled in the delicate handling required by the white glazed face brick used over the entire exterior. "Of course it goes more slowly, as is true for any specialized art," says Mr. Broff, "but we calculated for this timing at the outset."[197]

Despite this assertion of standards especially concerning the bricklaying, it was necessary for the two buildings to be reclad in 2001. Cutsogeorge Tooman & Allen, architects for the buildings at that time, found water penetration so severe that some of the white glazed brick had to be removed on an emergency basis. The original cavity wall construction was improperly handled. Outer glazed brick walls gradually expand over many freeze and thaw cycles, while gravity compresses the inner walls. The zinc ties between them were failing. Craig Tooman reports that

> . . . we were forced to provide support for the back-up masonry that was overhanging the slab edges, an original condition, and a very poor installation. Added to this was the

---

[196] "35 East 85th Street," *Real Estate Forum*, pp. 57-58.

[197] *Ibid.*, pp. 58-60.

use of improper shimming of the shelf angles at every floor
using pieces of electrical conduit and other inappropriate
materials. Together these two conditions would have forced
us to install a wide band of new brick at every floor around
the full perimeter of the building. Once this was determined
it became a relatively logical choice to rebrick the entire
building and avoid future problems with the glazed brick.[198]

Cutsogeorge Tooman & Allen believe that the contractor rather
than the original architects are at fault for inadequate supervision of
subcontractors of the various components. Speed was valued over
attention to detail.

The remedial work did not determine what brick should replace the
original white brick. The choice of red brick was made by the board of
the cooperative:

In the past decade when moisture afflicted 35 East 85th
Street and 400 East 85th Street, both buildings elected to
ditch their white bricks, choosing red-brick facades that
alluded to Georgian architecture.

"As we went through the design process, the boards got
unanimous feedback from brokers that a change to red brick
would increase the value of their apartments," said Craig
Tooman . . .

Proponents of white brick – and they do exist – find the
redos disheartening. "When buildings replace white brick
with red brick and a full historical limestone base, I see
people who are defeated and don't believe in the future,"
said Françoise Bollack, an architect and an associate professor
at Columbia University. "They want something that looks

---

[198] Correspondence with the author, May 20, 2010.

historic because they think it's classy. In 20 years, they'll regret it."[199]

Excavation for The Hawthorne for David Rose & Associates, at 211 East 53rd Street (1958-60), posed a special problem:

The Hawthorne, 211 East 53rd Street, and Second Avenue, 1958-60.

The site bridged a sort of underground canyon, with a precipice of schist on the westerly side and, on the easterly end, Turtle Bay Creek gurgling its subterranean way to the

---

[199]   "White Brick Tiptoes Into the Sun," *The New York Times*, May 16, 2010, Real Estate, p. 9.

East River many feet below the surface. As a result, blasting in one part of the plot had to be matched with pile driving at another.[200]

An innovative technique was used here: pre-welded mats were positioned instead of hand-tying the steel rods into mesh on-site. Concrete could be poured immediately on positioning the mats, and this saved 15 cents per square foot or $21,000 in the Hawthorne apartments.[201]

The facade is more articulated than many of the Boak & Raad commissions for Rose Associates:

> The front wall masonry employs two shades of gray glazed brick, one very light and the other somewhat darker, the darker being used on the protruding center portion and the lighter on both sides thereof. However, the central pier of the center portion is of the lighter shade, but employs a moulded curvilinear rather than a standard rectangular brick, laid in stacked bond -- the rest of the brickwork being in conventional running bond.[202]

Piers of stacked moulded brick was a favorite device used in the pre-war Boak & Paris buildings. Also at the Hawthorne, the forward-thrust affords corner windows as in their prewar buildings.

In its 14 stories, the Hawthorne has 145 apartments, from two to six rooms with many luxury features: "In addition to sizable rooms, the atmosphere of spaciousness is enhanced in most of the apartments by adept employment of layout design. For example, even in a number of the smaller apartments, the living rooms are flanked with dining alcoves and foyers which are so arranged as to create a diagonal vista well in

---

[200] "The Hawthorne," *Real Estate Forum*, August 1959, pp. 28-41.

[201] *The New York Times*, April 26, 1959, Real Estate. p. 6.

[202] "The Hawthorne," *Real Estate Forum*, August 1959, p. 36.

excess of what would otherwise be available with the square footage employed."[203]

"The lobby concept at The Hawthorne, as created by Intramural, Inc., Beryl S. Austrian, A.I.D., president, uses a contemporary interpretation of neo-classic, a style typical of the original Turtle Bay residences near the new building."[204]

The years 1958-61 were very productive for Boak & Raad, with substantial corner or blockfront buildings of similar design: buildings of greater width than height; facades dominated by horizontal strips of windows; height culminating in setbacks and terraces. For Seidman-Soling Builders, they did two red brick buildings, 136 East 76th Street at Lexington Avenue (1958-61), 15 stories and penthouse, and The Gaylord at 251 East 51st Street at Second Avenue (1959-60). At the 76th Street building,

> Two "consumer angles" will be offered; to wit, Park Ave. area quarters will be made available at Third Ave. rates, and use of the steel frame in lieu of the more usual reinforced concrete will enable 8'6" ceilings and greater floor area because of smaller interior projections, including columns.[205]

The grocery store, D'Agostino's rented the full Lexington Avenue frontage. The second floor was for professional offices with an entrance separate from the main entrance. The apartments are from three to six rooms, with most above the eleventh floor terraced. The lobby design was by Intramural, Inc.

---

[203] *Ibid.*, p. 37.

[204] *Ibid.*, p. 36. This article deals with the Hawthorne and also the Brookford, built by Rose Associates at 65 Park Terrace West in the Inwood section of Manhattan. Atypically, this article does not mention the architect of either building; Leo Stillman was the architect of the Brookford. A plaque on the front of the Hawthorne reads: "ERECTED 1960/ROSE ASSOCIATES BUILDERS/BOAK & RAAD ARCHITECTS."

[205] *Real Estate Forum*, May 1960, p. 17.

Irving Seidman and Chester Soling had purchased the plot at 51ˢᵗ Street and Second Avenue from Minskoff & Sons.[206] As at the Hawthorne, the pesky Turtle Bay Creek ran through the site, making it necessary to shore up adjacent buildings.[207] The Gaylord is taller, at 19 stories plus penthouses, than their 15-story 76ᵗʰ Street building. It also rests on a small base of 100 feet x 150 feet and rises 176 feet, so its four stories of setbacks give it a more tapering silhouette than many of Boak & Raad's other buildings.

While many feature articles in the *Real Estate Forum* include studio photographs of the owners and the architects, it is only in the feature article about the Gaylord in 1960 that there is a photograph of Russell Boak. It is not a studio portrait; he and Chester Soling are shown "hold[ing] progress talk at the building."[208] These *Real Estate Forum* articles mentioned all the contractors and suppliers involved in the project, and in turn the contractors and suppliers took ads. Until fairly recently, it was considered unprofessional for architects, like their fellow professionals doctors and lawyers, to advertise. Boak carried this to an extreme in never including a studio portrait in these feature articles – or else he was modest or shy.

---

[206] *The New York Times*, September 20, 1959, Real Estate, p. 14.

[207] "The Gaylord," *Real Estate Forum*, August 1960, pp. 44-53.

[208] *Ibid.*, p. 48. See Chapter 12 for this photo.

CHAPTER 10

Midcentury Modern and White Brick

Simon Brothers were the builders for the owner Sylvia Rifka of 130 East 63rd Street at Lexington (1958-60), "Inside the Social Sixties . . . in the new Beekman Hill School District." The Boak & Raad building has a facade of white glazed brick with granite facing on the first floor. There are stores on the Lexington Avenue frontage. Its height is 14 stories plus penthouse, its terraces and setbacks starting at the eleventh floor. In this building, the lobby was designed by Raymond Loewy.[209]

East 47th Street was widened from Second to First Avenue and renamed Dag Hammarsjkold Plaza to create a ceremonial mall leading to the United Nations. Embassy House anchors this plaza at the northeast corner of 47th Street and extends to 48th Street on Second Avenue.[210]

---

[209] *The New York Times*, October 16, 1960, Real Estate, p. 9.

[210] *The New York Times*, October 23, 1958, p. 52.

Embassy House, 301 East 47th Street, 1958-61.

The entrance to 301 East 47th Street is from the plaza. Boak & Raad designed this luxury building for Geller and Mitchell in 1958, completed in 1961. Because of its location north of the plaza, Embassy House could "offer a panoramic view of the East River and the UN buildings through picture windows of up to 16-1/2 feet in many apartments with many living rooms as large as 30 feet."[211]

Embassy House has 288 apartments and stands 20 stories plus penthouses with setbacks and terraces. These form two towers as observed from Second Avenue. The sections between the towers are recessed from the street plane. It is faced with a light tan brick, with

---

[211]   *Real Estate Forum*, November 1961, p. 7.

windows grouped in single, double and triple units. There are stores on the Second Avenue side.

The luxury apartment building at Eight East 83rd Street (1960-63) exemplifies Boak & Raad's ingenuity and pragmatism, according to *The New York Times* story headlined "Zoning and Codes Test Architects: Designs Turn Restrictions into Building Assets." In 1961 changes were made to the 1916 zoning regulations governing the height at which buildings were required to set back. "The architects, Boak & Raad, found that a portion of the plot -- forty feet at its easterly end -- was within 100 feet of Madison Avenue," which meant it was permissible to build that section to 16 stories, while the westerly portion was limited to 14 stories.[212]

The building had 84 units, of four to seven rooms each. The builder, Joseph P. Blitz, publicized its central air conditioning, automatic dishwashers, wall ovens, and an underground garage. Other luxury features included separate apartments for the maids of tenants, bay windows and wood-burning fireplaces.[213] The multiple setbacks provided terraces for many of the apartments, some of which were duplexes. Four maisonettes were also duplexes, entered by a landscaped walk "made possible by setting the structure back from the building line."[214] It is another of the white brick facade buildings.

Hemisphere House is a 19-story building on the eastern blockfront of Sixth Avenue from 56th to 57th Street. Boak & Raad designed 60 West 57th Street for Andros Realty Corporation, with the new building permit filed in 1960 and completed in late 1963. News stories at that time highlighted measures taken to diminish noise between apartments and from plumbing, and the return of elegance in the lobby through extensive use of marble.[215] The building was long in gestation, as Boak & Raad had filed a New Building permit for this site and this owner on July 24,

---

[212]   *The New York Times*, February 3, 1962, p. 45.

[213]   *The New York Times*, June 30, 1963, p. 8.

[214]   "News of New Buildings," *Real Estate Forum*, March 1963, p. 44.

[215]   *The New York Times*, June 9, 1963, p. 351 and December 22, 1963, p. W 4.

1944. A rendering dated September 8, 1944 for an 18-story blockfront apartment building may be an early design for Hemisphere House.

Early design (1944) of Hemisphere House,
60 West 57th Street, and Sixth Avenue; actually built, 1960-63.

It shows details used by Boak & Paris prior to the war: corner casement windows, vertical piers and Greek key emblems up to the beginning of the setbacks. None of these is present in the 1960s building, but the height and massing are similar, with a bold bandcourse above the ground floor stores and recessed planes on the facades.

Marble figured prominently in another Andros-Boak & Raad joint project. In 1962, Andros Broadway, Inc. started a renovation of 29 Broadway, a 31-story office building by Sloan & Robinson of 1929-31. It was long the home of major shipping companies, so when Holland-America Lines moved out, there was an opportunity to renovate the lower four floors and integrate the adjacent six-story structure at 31-33 Broadway. "A marble, granite and brick facade has always been one of the features most prized by the owners," so creating a unified facade was complicated by the fact that the original quarry had closed. "A long search followed this discovery, according to John Avlon, Inc., the renting agent."[216] Marble was found in Alabama which closely matched the original New York State marble. The granite and gray brick was less of a problem. The Boak & Raad addition is definitely subordinate to the highly ornamented main entry, but complements it.

Boak & Raad were the architects of a 1963 addition to the Bing & Bing building at Two Horatio Street at Greenwich Avenue, of which by Robert T. Lyons was the original architect. This had been part of Bing & Bing's ambitious Greenwich Village construction project of 1929, in which Boak & Paris were the architects of 302 West 12th Street and 45 Christopher Street. Their extension is respectful of the Lyons' original, matching floor levels and the height of the windows, and extending the trim. But it is easy to distinguish the prewar and postwar sections because the windows in the older section are uniformly two casements side by side, while in the newer section there is a variety of window units: strips of two casements on either side of a fixed window, single casements flanking one fixed window, and two casements like the original.

The firm of Rose Associates included David Rose and his three nephews Frederick P., Daniel and Elihu who

> have carried on their uncle's pioneering tradition. For example, they entered a field where few private developers have been active — the construction of middle-income housing under the Limited Profit Housing Companies

---

[216] *The New York Times*, June 28, 1964, Real Estate, p. 1.

program, or Mitchell-Lama program as it is popularly called. In 1963 the firm embarked on one of the most extensive building programs under that program, constructing 2500 units in the next two years.[217]

Boak & Raad were the architects of one of these Mitchell-Lama projects, Leland House, two 22-story buildings at 910-920 and 945-955 Underhill Avenue, in the Bronx, completed in 1964.

Leland House in Schuyler Village, 945-955 Underhill Avenue and 910-930 Thieriot Avenue, Bronx, New York, 1961-64.

The site is a superblock running from Bruckner Boulevard to Story Avenue, Underhill to Thieriot Avenues, of which the northwest corner is for parking and the southeast corner is garden area. These towers in the park buildings are straight-line, doubled-loaded slabs oriented north-south, but offset on the site to minimize the shadow one would cast on the other. They are rescued from anonymity by the use of gray

---

217   "Rose Luxury Apartment Program Largest in City," *Real Estate Forum*, November 1966, p. 62. The luxury buildings that were the primary topic of this article are the Churchill and Georgetown Plaza, neither of which were designed by Boak & Raad.

and green brick, and by slightly recessed and projecting planes -- similar to the Hawthorne in midtown Manhattan -- as well as balconies for most units. Despite the fact that Mitchell-Lama projects were built for families with limited incomes, the apartments have rooms of nearly the same size as those in luxury buildings Rose Associates was erecting about the same time, Georgetown Plaza at 60 East Eighth Street, Leo Stillman and John Pruyn, architects, and the Churchill, at Second Avenue from East 39th to 40th Streets, Philip Birnbaum, architect. The public areas of Leland House were designed by the same interior designer, Intramural Inc., Beryl S. Austrian, President, who designed those of Rose luxury buildings.[218]

Boak & Raad were the architects of the Murray Park, at 120 East 34th Street between Park and Lexington Avenues, built by Algin Management.

---

[218]   *Real Estate Forum*, July 1964, p. 8.

The Murray Park, 120 East 34th Street, and Lexington Avenue, 1964.

It is clad in their familiar red brick. This was the home of Ayn Rand from 1965 until her death in 1982. She had become famous for her novels *The Fountainhead* (1943) and *Atlas Shrugged* (1957). The Murray Park "was her last and longest address. Her husband Frank O'Connor, a painter, also rented a small apartment in the building just to paint in. Nathaniel and Barbara Branden also lived there, and for a while the offices of *The Objectivist* magazine and Nathaniel Branden Institute were on the second floor."[219]

---

[219] Email message to author from Fred Cookinham, June 2, 2012.

In 1956 when the Minskoffs erected the Brevoort facing Fifth Avenue, they had also leased from Sailors Snug Harbor the eastern part of that block fronting on University Place from Eighth to Ninth Streets. This foresight allowed them to set rents at the Brevoort East, 20 East Ninth Street, when it was completed in 1965 at the same scale as the Brevoort, even though construction costs had risen approximately 25 percent in the intervening decade.

Brevoort East, 20 East Ninth Street, and University Place, 1961-65.

The feature article in the *Real Estate Forum* notes that "A highly rated talent in luxury apartment building design, Russell M. Boak, drew the plans for Brevoort East . . . Brevoort East is marked by simplicity of design, with an 11-story tower sitting atop a base structure of 15 floors."[220]

The Brevoort East is not only taller than the Breevort, it is also bulkier, filling out its envelope more completely. Still the lower section has north and south wings with a private courtyard between them, and the tower is recessed from the University Place front. Like the Brevoort, there are corner balconies and corner casement windows at recessed locations.

The Brevoort faces Fifth Avenue, and in order to leave the noise of the avenue behind, its entrance is recessed with a porte cochere, with landscaping framing its driveway. In order to accommodate stores on its University Place and Eighth Street fronts, the Brevoort East could not be simply a mirror image of the Brevoort. The entry is moved to the quieter side street, Ninth Street. It is designed with care. The sidewalk outside the outer door has a pattern which is continued in marble into the lobby. Through the large glass doors can be seen a mural of 19th century Greenwich Village and the Washington Square Arch. Large windows light the lobby and give a view of a garden area just west of the lobby.

The rental brochure for the Brevoort East -- "Proud heir to an illustrious name at Washington Square" -- is big, slick and 20 pages; the photo on the cover is of the Washington Square Arch rather than the new building, and throughout it evokes Greenwich Village history as often as the modernity of the new building. The tone is almost defensive. One bit of local color is omitted from the brochure: the Brevoort East

---

[220] "Current Program Enhances Minskoff Prestige: Brevoort East Suites Draw Widespread Praise; Avenue of Americas Skyscraper Scores Success," *Real Estate Forum*, April 1966, pp.41-53. The article notes that "In the past ten years, the Minskoffs have shifted some of their realty construction talent toward office buildings."

stands on the former site of the Cedar Tavern, the erstwhile hangout of the Abstract Expressionists, which moved north on University Place.

Raad retired in 1965 while the Brevoort East was under construction. The firm as Russell M. Boak Associates maintained its office at the Flatiron Building, 175 Fifth Avenue.[221] The firm designed another building for Rose Associates,

> The Homestead, a 7-story apartment building overlooking the fairways and lakes of the Scarsdale Country Club, at 80 East Hartsdale Ave., Hartsdale . . . The 170-unit building was designed with emphasis on the attractive views surrounding the building and privacy within each apartment, according to Russell M. Boak, the architect. Oversize picture windows and windows with large sliding panels have been used throughout the building, instead of the usual double-hung windows. In several lines of apartments that have balconies, floor-to-ceiling sliding glass doors provide entry from living rooms or dining areas. For privacy, most apartments have distinct foyers that prevent the entire living room from being exposed when the front door is opened.[222]

The pendulum had swung back: separate foyers were prized in prewar buildings, then combined with living rooms and even with living-dining rooms in the postwar era, and now are reintroduced.

Boak worked on another project with Rose Associates, Tower 53 at Seventh Avenue and 53rd Street in 1965-67.

---

[221] New York Telephone Directories, 1966-72.

[222] "Construction and Modernization," *Real Estate Forum*, April 1966, p. 16.

Tower 53, 825 Seventh Avenue and 159 West 53rd Street, 1965-67.

In 1965 when Loew's Theatres and Hotels commissioned Tower 53, Seventh Avenue was rather run-down, but Eero Saarinen's CBS Building was being completed on 53rd and Sixth Avenue, so they hoped to succeed with a mixed-use building. Rose Associates acted as owners' consultant. This 37-story white-brick building has ten floors of offices, which use the address of 825 Seventh Avenue, and apartments above, with the address of 159 West 53rd Street. The 216 apartments range in size from studios to 7-1/2 rooms. On 53rd Street, the apartment tower is set back from the office base, which protects its light and buffers street noise. Chevron-shaped balconies with glass screens are staggered on the Seventh Avenue facade.[223]

At 357 feet, Tower 53 is the tallest building by Boak, but does not appear particularly tall, partly because it is in a business district with taller buildings. Tower 53 does not have the tapering wedding-cake silhouette of setbacks and terraces of the Boak & Paris towers of the 1930s. After the 1961 zoning changes, providing public plazas earned height bonuses, and Tower 53 has a modest plaza on the Seventh Avenue side.

The brochure for Tower 53 says it offers "a combination of convenience and luxury for those whose interests or activities center in this area," and that the

> Apartments at Tower 53 encompass an unusually broad spectrum of layouts and arrangements. Studio suites include dining foyers and spacious sleeping areas; a number have balconies. Many one and two bedroom apartments have balconies and a number of one bedroom apartments also

---

[223] Similar balconies were used on Plaza Tower at 118 East 60th Street, a 34-story building for which Boak & Raad received a New Building permit in 1961. Samuel Paul and Seymour Jarmul were the architects; *The New York Times*, March 7, 1965. Similar balconies are also used on Plaza 400, 400 East 56th Street and First Avenue, the Philip Birnbaum design of 1965 which replaced Boak & Raad's design for the eastern end of the Doelger block. All are called "Plaza" presumably because the buildings are set back from their lot lines and therefore received a bonus of additional height.

have powder rooms. Upper-floor duplexes [38th-39th floors] of 5 and 7-1/2 rooms have unusually spacious private terraces with breathtaking views.[224]

Bernard Strassner, then Chief Engineer for Rose Associates, recalls the care Russell Boak took in distinguishing the commercial and residential lobbies which are connected by an inconspicuous door. The entrance for the offices is on Seventh Avenue, and the lobby is modern, while the apartment entrance is on the side street and is of more traditional design. He points out that Boak used some Art Deco details such as the Greek key – "Boak's signature" – and his buildings were never just plain boxes. Trim and window treatments raise the price, which developers tend to resist, according to Strassner.[225]

In 1968, Russell M. Boak Associates filed a New Building permit for 60 East End Avenue. However, on its completion in 1973, the rental brochure attributes it to Philip Birnbaum.[226]

Boak was going blind when he closed his architectural practice about 1972.[227] The city's declining economic outlook may also have played a part in the decision. He and his wife continued to live at the Westmore until his death in 1981.[228] Thomas Raad, who lived in Forest Hills, Queens, also died in 1981.

*   *   *

---

[224] Brochure for Tower 53, author's collection.

[225] Telephone conversation with the author, December 11, 2002.

[226] Brochure in Sylvan and Robert L. Bien archives, Avery Architectural and Fine Arts Library, Columbia University.

[227] Conversation with Bruce Schlecter, Rose Associates, June 18, 2002.

[228] Conversation with Charles Lako, superintendent of the Westmore, August 10, 2000. Boak spent his last days in the Mary Manning Walsh Nursing Home, Manhattan, and is buried in Woodlawn Cemetery in the Bronx, as are his parents and sister Mildred.

The postwar apartment houses brought heavy criticism from Lewis Mumford writing in 1950 of "The Plight of the Prosperous":

> For a long time I have been wanting to say a word about the apartment buildings that have sprung up since the war in the wealthy and fashionable parts of the city, mainly on and near upper Park Avenue and Fifth Avenue . . . While all over town the New York City Housing Authority has been erecting, for the low-income group, skyscraper apartments that provide light and air and walks and sometimes even patches of grass and forsythia, the quarters for the prosperous are still being put up with positive contempt for the essentials of good housing . . .

Mumford said of one new building that the interior, "'like the interiors of all the neighboring buildings, has been governed by only one consideration, maximum coverage of the land,' resulting in a lack of cross ventilation, a comparatively small number of units with southern exposure and oddly proportioned rooms."[229]

Thomas A. Creighton, editor of *Progressive Architecture*, wrote in 1961 "Twice each day I walk through the devastation of the upper East Side, where block after block of reasonably well-designed buildings is being torn down and replaced with unrelated brick 'luxury' apartments – boxes with air holes in them."[230]

In 1969 the Landmarks Preservation Commission report on the Greenwich Village Historic District was written, which celebrates the Greek revival row houses extant in the Village. This report is so negative about Boak & Raad's Brevoort and Brevoort East for the Minskoffs that it does not even deign to name the architects:

---

[229] "The Sky Line: The Plight of the Prosperous," *New Yorker*, March 4, 1950, pp. 68-73, quoted in *New York 1960*, pp. 799-800.

[230] "P.S.: Happy New York," editorial, *Progressive Architecture*, January 1961, p. 208, quoted in *New York 1960*, p. 800.

This gigantic double apartment house, with its windows stressing the horizontal, is a brash intruder lacking the features which might retain any kinship whatsoever with its handsome neighbors across the street. Obviously no design controls were exercised here, and the result is a building which in every way defies its surroundings.[231]

In fairness, the Brevoort does little to acknowledge its other neighbor, the building across Fifth Avenue -- 20 Fifth Avenue, the Modern Classical Boak & Paris building of 1939-40. They differ in materials, windows and ornamentation. However, the setbacks of the two buildings start at about the same height probably due to the zoning.

In recent years, there has been a re-evaluation of postwar apartment houses. As an indication of how tastes change, in 2002 the Brevoort was listed among "New York's Most Desirable Glazed-Brick Buildings," in *The New York Times Magazine*. The other three buildings listed are 812 Fifth Avenue (1961; Robert Bien); Manhattan House, 200 East 66th Street (1950, Skidmore, Owings & Merrill and Mayer & Whittlesey); and Imperial House, 150 East 69th Street (1958, Emery Roth & Sons).

The main article described architect Kimberly Ackert's radical alterations to a Fifth Avenue apartment including combining rooms and creating wider windows to open up the view of Central Park.

Ackert's clients actually liked the building because its postwar modernity lent itself to the kind of contemporary design aesthetic they sought for their own living spaces. Never mind that buildings of this vintage have fairly awkward proportions, being generally wider than they are tall; that was the architect's challenge.

But lesser white-brick buildings without prime views have also become more popular because of changing aesthetics:

---

[231] Landmarks Preservation Commission Greenwich Village Historic District Designation Report [LP 0489], New York, City of New York, 1969, Area 1, p. 37

In the past few years, midcentury furniture and design have had a renaissance. This has given a sheen to the angular 60's buildings, most of which have eight-foot ceilings, boxy rooms and little detail . . . Jeffrey Bilhuber [interior decorator said that] "modern furniture profiles much lower to the floor, which looks fantastic in a 60's era space."[232]

As discerning a critic as Terence Riley, then chief curator of architecture and design at the Museum of Modern Art, chose a 1960 H. I. Feldman building on West 12th Street for the same reason. He said there was "no question" that he wanted a minimalist 60's building when he went apartment shopping. "I can't tell you how long I looked for an eight-foot ceiling."[233]

Such buildings are favored for their interiors and/or their views rather than for their exteriors. The interiors are often so plain that their occupants and especially their decorators feel free to treat them as blank slates rather than conserving original details and proportions. Removing walls to combine living and dining rooms and kitchens are frequent alterations – in contrast to practices of the 1930s when architects like Boak & Paris broke up the large apartments of the 1920s and earlier to create smaller apartments, but usually keeping separate rooms for living, dining and cooking.

How then shall these postwar buildings be rated? Paul Goldberger gave voice to our ambivalence about these apartment buildings:

Modernism is history, and has to be appreciated as such. Even apart from the Trade Center and the emotional impact of September 11th, I sense that today, there is a pretty broad willingness to admit that. My sense is that the great buildings of modern architecture in New York - the Ford Foundations

---

[232] Pilar Viladas, "Traveling Light," *The New York Times Magazine*, March 3, 2002, pp. 71-78.

[233] "A Haven for Women Is No Longer Quite Home," *The New York Times*, January 13, 2002, Section 9, p. 1.

and TWAs and Seagrams and Levers – are not the issue. Most of them are landmarks, or will be, and so will most of the things shown in this exhibition. There is no disputing their quality, and their importance. The problem is the next layer down, and our discomfort with a lot of what was built in the nineteen-fifties and sixties. The reality is that modernism did not create a decent vernacular - that was, in fact, its problem. It could more easily create great individual works than an urban fabric, so there was no modern equivalent of the brownstone, or the great apartment houses of the twenties, that everyone could jointly admire and feel comfortable about preserving. And if I can end on a note of uncertainty, I am still not entirely sure what to do about this, since the towers of Third Avenue and Sixth Avenue or the white-brick apartment buildings of Second Avenue are not great buildings, however important they are to the historical context of the city, and neither do most of them have the powerful iconic status that the World Trade Center had, even before its loss. Yet neither do we want to see all of them disappear.[234]

---

[234] Speech, November 14, 2001, in conjunction with exhibition "Modern Architecture on the Upper East Side: Landmarks of the Future" at New York School of Interior Design, 2001-02.

CHAPTER 11

Trying to Make It with Commercial Projects

Prewar and postwar, the firm Boak & Paris and Boak & Raad made its mark designing apartment buildings, but had ambitions to do commercial work as well. Especially after the war, it seemed that commercial work would be more lucrative than residential work. Emery Roth's sons did fewer residential designs and became major designers of commercial skyscrapers. Among the major clients of Boak & Raad, the Minskoffs moved boldly into commercial real estate. Rose Associates, however, did only two commercial buildings in Manhattan, 280 Park Avenue and 1180 Sixth Avenue, neither of which was designed by Boak & Raad. Russell Boak and Thomas Raad tried to be players in this game. But in the end, for reasons beyond their control, the proposed big developments did not materialize, and their commercial projects that did get built were modest in scale.

Where their apartment buildings faced on avenues zoned for stores on the ground floor, many of their buildings had the retail businesses that residential neighborhoods need – grocery stores, shoe repair shops, cleaners and the like. Boak & Paris had a few single-purpose commercial buildings, most notably the Midtown, now Metro, Theater, discussed in Chapter 3. There is also the restaurant building for Howard Johnson in 1939, which continues today as the steakhouse Maloney & Porcelli (see Chapter 6). The last building of Russell Boak, Tower 53, discussed in Chapter 10, exemplifies a new kind of hybrid structure, residential floors above a substantial number of commercial floors, enough that the building has separate entrances and elevators to serve the two functions.

As with residential buildings, so with commercial buildings, Sam Minskoff and then Sam Minskoff & Sons were major clients of the firm. In the Bronx in 1939, Sam Minskoff had Boak & Paris do a one-story commercial building at 1200 Grant Avenue and 167th Street (see Chapter 5). There were a number of one- and two-story taxpayers for the Sons in Queens – in Jackson Heights, Kew Gardens, Rego Park and Forest Hills (1947-49). There is a similar building at Vanderbilt Avenue and Park Place in Brooklyn (1952). Typically these were retail, with offices on the second floor if they were two story.

In White Plains, Minskoff commissioned a one-story taxpayer at Mamaroneck and Martine Avenues in 1939. Postwar, the Minskoffs had them design a 13-unit shopping center at Martine Avenue and Court Street, and two structures on East Post Road near Mamaroneck Avenue (1947-52). An office building for the Improved Risk Mutuals, owned jointly by 11 mutual life insurance companies, made its headquarters at 15 North Broadway, on a sale-lease transaction with Sam Minskoff & Sons, builders (1952). Boak & Raad used a modified Georgian style for the building.

The most ambitious of the White Plains commercial buildings for the Minskoffs is the office building at 55 Church Street, heralded in a story on the front page of the Real Estate section of *The New York Times* in late 1952:

> As further indication of the continued demand for business space in communities close to New York, Sam Minskoff & Sons, Inc., builders, announced plans yesterday for the erection of a large air-conditioned office building in the heart of the commercial district in White Plains.
>
> The Westchester structure will be six stories in height, modern in style, and will represent an investment of nearly $2,000,000, according to Henry Minskoff, president of the New York company.

55 Church Street, White Plains, 1952-54.

> Mr. Minskoff said the project was undertaken to meet
> the needs of nationally known organizations desiring to rent
> rather than to build their own office facilities in the busy
> White Plains area . . . the first major project of its kind in
> that section since World War II.[235]

The rendering that appeared with the article showed six stories, but
as built it is only four. It has features associated with the International
Style – continuous strip windows, and pilotis at the entrance, which is
in the center of the building.

Irving Maidman announced in 1947 that he planned to build a bus
terminal, garage and office building from 42nd to 43rd Streets, west of
Eighth Avenue, with Boak & Raad as architects. This would have been
just north of the Port Authority Union Bus Terminal also proposed at
this time. "The architects' plans provide for adding 22 floors of office
space to the base structure at a future date when building materials are
available." A Boak & Raad drawing shows only eight bays for buses.

---

[235] "New Offices Will Rise in White Plains; Minskoffs Planning Air-Cooled
Building," *The New York Times*, November 30, 1952, Real Estate, p. 1.

The Port Authority did build its bus terminal, but Maidman did not: he had two more architects draw up plans before finally abandoning the project in 1948.[236]

At 804 Lexington Avenue and 64th Street, there is a two-story building dating from 1937-38 with the entrance at the chamfered corner. In fact this shape is the prototype of almost all the little retail buildings throughout the firm's existence. One of these stood at 888 Madison Avenue and 72nd Street from 1951 to 2008. This had been the site of a McKim, Mead & White mansion from which Consuelo Vanderbilt was married. The Boak & Raad taxpayer housed Ralph Lauren Sports until it was demolished for a grande luxe limestone and marble palazzo for Ralph Lauren Womenswear and Home.[237]

One Boak & Raad shopping center built by Sidney and Arthur Diamond received an award from the Queens Chamber of Commerce for "excellence in design and construction" in 1951.[238] It is situated across from Parkway Village, at Main Street, 79th Avenue and 146th Street in Kew Garden Hills. The one-story building contains 30,000 square feet with nearly 30,000 square feet set aside for off-street parking, then a relatively new concept.[239]

Roseland was a dance hall from the 1920s until it closed in 2014. In 1956 Roseland moved to 239 West 52nd Street, once the Gay Blades ice skating rink.[240] Boak & Raad prepared two designs, one for a roller skating rink which would have continued the Gay Blades name

---

236   *Real Estate Record and Guide*, March 8, 1947, p. 3. Also April 3, 1948, pp. 3-4, and September 11, 1948, p. 5.

237   Christopher Gray, "Streetscapes: From Palatial Home to Retail Palace," *The New York Times*, March 16, 2008, Real Estate, p. 7; also "Streetscapes: From a Mysterious Mansion to a Ralph Lauren Store," *The New York Times*, October 7, 2010.

238   *The New York Times*, December 3, 1951, Real Estate, p. 48.

239   *The New York Times*, November 5, 1950, p. 229.

240   *The New York Times*, July 24, 1981.

and another for "The New Roseland Ballroom."[241] The facade of the Roseland that closed in 2014 does not resemble either drawing.

Boak & Raad have only one public commission in New York City, the Forest Hills Branch of the Queens Borough Public Library.

Forest Hills Branch of the Queens Borough Public Library,
108-19 71st Avenue, 1957-58.

This library "had been forced out of its home in August, reopened on November 3, 1946, in a 'temporary' building at 108-19 71st Avenue, erected through public subscription. A permanent home for the branch was not built for another decade."[242] Indeed a rendering of the Boak & Raad design is dated 1948,[243] while the cornerstone is dated 1957 and

---

[241]   Renderings in the Wurts Collection at the Museum of the City of New York.

[242]   Jeffey A. Kroessler, *Lighting the Way: The Centennial History of the Queens Borough Public Library, 1896-1996* (New York: The Donning Company Publishers, 1996), p. 109.

[243]   Photo by Wurts Brothers, Collection of the Museum of the City of New York, negative 817545.

the commemorative plaque inside is dated 1958. It stands two stories high, with an auditorium in the basement. A center section, which protrudes slightly, houses its entrance and stairs. The library is clad in red brick, with light cast stone window enframements.

In early 1950, Boak & Raad were the architects of the projected Mount Vernon Terminal Shopping Center

> to occupy space now covered by present railroad station and parking area. It will have thirty-eight stories, 600-seat theatre, railroad ticket office and roof parking. The site extends from Third Avenue to Park Avenue and from Prospect Avenue to the New Haven tracks.[244]

In a *Real Esate Forum* article mostly about their apartment building at 440 East 56th Street, there is mention of this "much discussed railroad station development in Mt. Vernon for the New York, New Haven & Hartford Railroad."[245]

They seemed to be developing a reputation for shopping centers, to judge from a 1952 statement in *Real Estate Forum*:

> The firm has been active in recent years in designing a number of shopping centers, including one in Bristol, Pa., another one on North Avenue in New Rochelle, in addition to the White Plains office for the Improved Risk Mutual Insurance Company, and another office building in Syracuse.[246]

Still another project involving the New York, New Haven & Hartford Railroad was announced in 1956, to be built at the New Rochelle station. It would include a railroad station, hotel, shopping

---

[244]   *The New York Times*, February 26, 1950, Real Estate, p. 1.

[245]   *Real Estate Forum*, October 1950, p. 20.

[246]   *Real Estate Forum*, September 1952, p. 21.

center and parking, at a cost of $17 million.[247] By September 1957, the project, now called Westchester Terminal Plaza, had grown to $41 million, still with Boak & Raad as the architects.[248] In 1958, the cost was still estimated at $41 million, but now the architect was Victor Gruen, a much better known designer of shopping malls.[249] By January 1961, Westchester Plaza was somewhat scaled back to an estimated cost of $27 million, but now John Graham & Company was listed as architect.[250] Ground was broken on December 28, 1961.[251]

However, after repeated contract defaults by the development corporation, the city of New Rochelle cancelled the sale of the land:

> Not a single major structure has been begun, although the 18-acre downtown site has been cleared. Macy's and Sears, Roebuck & Co. were reported by officials as being still interested in big stores on the tract. The New Haven Railroad, uncertain of its future, showed no continuing interest in the project.[252]

Indeed, the railroad had been in bankruptcy since 1961, hurt by the loss of freight business to the new highways. Passenger traffic alone was not profitable enough to sustain the New Haven. Both the Mount Vernon and the New Rochelle projects seem to have been peripheral victims of the railroad's decline.

It seems fair to say that the enduring reputation of the firm of Boak & Paris/Boak & Raad will depend on its residential work rather than on its commercial work.

---

247 *The New York Times*, August 14, 1956, p. 20, news story, and August 16, 1956, p. 27, illustrations.

248 *Real Estate Forum*, September 1957, p. 10.

249 *Real Estate Forum*, July 1958, p. 10.

250 *Real Estate Forum*, January 1961, p. 6.

251 *The New York Times*, December 28, 1961. Also *Real Estate Forum*, February 1962, p. 64.

252 *The New York Times*, March 14, 1964.

Russell M. Boak and Chester Soling, 1960.

CHAPTER 12

Appreciations

Architects of apartment houses must compete within three closely-related circles. The first is the real estate owners who commission and construct the buildings. The second is the architectural community, colleagues and critics. The third is the public needing a place to live. In each of these arenas, Boak & Paris/Boak & Raad rate well.

Architects are artists who can only realize their works if someone hires them; hence the maxim "first land the job." The very fact that developers such as the Minskoffs, Bing & Bing, the Halls, the Roses, the Diamonds and the Broffs gave much repeat business to Boak & Paris and then to Boak & Raad indicates their satisfaction with the firm's designs.

In an era when owners advertised and publicized, while architects as professionals did neither, these real estate magnates placed stories about Boak & Paris projects in the *Real Estate Record and Guide* and the real estate section of *The New York Times*. Postwar in the *Real Estate Forum*, Boak & Raad buildings were the feature articles 13 times in 17 years, including four feature articles in 1955 alone.

These developers primarily built on their own account, expecting to own and manage the buildings for years to come. Speculative builders who plan to sell on completion might cut corners, but these investment builders were concerned about the long-term costs of maintaining their properties. What endeared Boak & Paris to these owners was their cooperation in achieving this efficiency. This was summarized in comments about Sam Minskoff's 50 East 78th Street:

> Building for investment rather than quick resale influenced both plan and construction, and minimum upkeep and slow obsolescence became important factors. In designing the building the type of apartments considered most rentable were first worked out, then costs were estimated, and final decisions as to materials and exterior design were made on the basis of these controlling elements.[253]

Philip Birnbaum, who said Boak claimed him as his protégé, designed some 300 buildings in Manhattan and Queens; his obituary notes that

> What made him so popular among developers was the efficiency of his apartment layouts. There was virtually no wasted floor space in his units, meaning that builders could fit more apartments on a floor. Because he tried to eliminate interior hallways, occupants also got more usable room. He said he designed for the people who lived in his buildings, not the elite.[254]

This efficiency links Birnbaum to Boak and to Roth; but unlike these predecessors, Birnbaum had "little critical acclaim; 'banal' was among the kinder words used to describe his work," quoting the *Times* obituary.

Efficiency was not the only characteristic of Boak buildings; they also had what Daniel Rose called "charm":

> He lived in one of his own buildings at 333 West 57th Street and took pleasure in it. It has Art Deco touches, but

---

[253]   *The Architectural Forum*, May 1937, p. 412.

[254]   *The New York Times*, November 28, 1996.

modified and gentle; it has charm. There is a real courtyard between the two buildings, 333 West 57th and 340 West 58th, not just an airshaft.

Mr. Rose also mentioned 20 East 68th Street with the Greek key element, which he identified as Boak's signature, and 215 East 79th Street, with corner casement windows and dropped living rooms. "It had an interesting facade. Boak had a sense of taste and style."

Daniel Rose also recalled that

> Russ Boak dressed handsomely, he was dapper. He was not tall or imposing. He wore subtly patterned shirts with an artistic touch, stylish shirts and ties, perhaps a pocket handkerchief. He was gentlemanly, unassertive, with piercing eyes. Boak's wife was prim, friendly, understated.[255]

Elihu Rose, Daniel's brother who was also a principal in Rose Associates, recalled that they would commission Russell Boak if it was planned to be a distinguished building. "Boak was an unsung architect who was incapable of doing a bad drawing, a bad design. No one is comparable. Boak just had taste, he had class."[256]

To appreciate Russell Boak's standing among architects one must start with Emery Roth. His regard for Boak can be inferred from the fact that Roth appointed him as associate with a 25 percent interest in the business from 1923 to 1927. Emery Roth's grandson, Richard Roth, Jr., FAIA, RIBA, (b. 1933) says that "I did not start working at Emery Roth until 1956 and do not remember my father [Richard Roth, Sr., 1904-87] ever talking about partners in the firm during the 20s. I do remember my father talking about Boak though. He was a big fan and

---

[255]   Daniel Rose, interview by the author, October 28, 2002.

[256]   Elihu Rose, interview by Andrew S. Dolkart, June 19, 2012, Avery Architectural and Fine Arts Library, Columbia University.

felt Boak was a fine designer. I had met Boak when the firm was Boak & Raad, but did not know him other than a brief meeting."[257]

The owners who hired Boak and Raad used other architects as well, including Richard Roth after his father Emery's retirement. Some of them also commissioned George F. Pelham II, Sugarman & Berger and George H. Miller. In the early 1950s, Sylvan Bien (1893-1959) sent his son Robert (1924-2002), then a draftsman just graduated from architectural school, to a meeting to discuss the postwar building boom. The participants included Rosario Candela (1890-1953), H. I. Feldman (1896-1981), Horace Ginsbern (1900-1969) and Boak. Robert Bien recalled the meeting as jovial, "they all knew one another."[258]

In his 1957 application for membership in the American Institute of Architects, Russell Boak listed as references the architects George H. Levy, Frank G. Ackerman, Milton Glass (1906-93), and Philip Birnbaum (1907-96), as well as the developer William E. P. Doelger (1901-92). Levy, Ackerman and Glass were already members of the AIA. Glass had once worked for Emery Roth.[259] He was chairman of the Board of Standards and Appeals in the administration of Mayor John Lindsay. (Glass and Levy were also references for Thomas Raad, applying for AIA membership at the same time.)

The work of Boak & Paris was featured in the architectural press of the day. *Architectural Forum* for May 1937 presented a round-up of "Apartment Houses 1937" with photos and text and included the Rockefeller Apartments as well as Boak & Paris' building at 50 East 78th Street for Sam Minskoff. Both of those buildings were also featured in the August 15, 1936 and the September 4, 1937 issues of *Real Estate Record*. In the 1937 issue of *Real Estate Record*, 5 Riverside Drive was also included with an exterior photo and three interior shots. *Architectural Record* of October 1937 featured 5 Riverside Drive for the Simon Brothers as "A Fireproof Apartment House," with an exterior photo

---

[257]   Richard Roth, e-mail to the author, October 28, 2001.

[258]   Robert Bien, interview by the author, January 27, 2002.

[259]   *Mansions in the Clouds*, p. 219.

and floor plans. *Pencil Points* (later *Progressive Architect*) for June 1938 illustrated the revolving door entrance of 5 Riverside as "Comparative Details" (See chapter 4 above).

Christopher Gray, the architectural historian who contributes the "Streetscapes" column to *The New York Times*, has written of Boak & Paris:

> Together the architects did two remarkable things: they survived and even prospered during the 1930's, when more established architects could not, and they developed an elegant model for the urbane but down-sized apartment building in Depression-era New York.[260]

Mr. Gray writes that when he was nine years old

> My mother found a compassionate landlord, William E. P. Doelger, who rented this single-mother-of-three-with-a-shaky-job an apartment at 440 East 56th Street. He had built it in 1950, and it remains a lonely exemplar of how modernism and humanism can coexist and even thrive . . .

> In 1945 Mr. Doelger announced plans to rebuild the brewery block with seven apartment houses, dead-simple modern, but oriented toward rear gardens with fountains and pools. His architect, Boak & Raad, set the orange brick buildings back slightly from the street, with saw-tooth facades giving every apartment three or four corner windows.

> Although he built his complex over several years, the coordination of light, air and gardens set Mr. Doelger's effort quite apart from the one-at-a-time, stand-alone model used by the typical developer . . .

---

[260] *The New York Times*, July 15, 2001, "2 Little-Known Architects of Distinctive Buildings," Real Estate, p. 7.

That early exposure to a sensitive hand in architecture
still forms my expectations today. Every time I walk past
Boak & Raad's elegantly off-hand gesture, I think of Mr.
Doelger and what he did for New York and for us.[261]

Boak & Paris and Boak & Raad buildings stand in the main
residential areas of Manhattan, and are strong contributors to historic
districts on the Upper East Side, Upper West Side and Greenwich
Village. Many of these buildings are now cooperatives (or, in a few
cases, condominiums), in which shareholders have a strong interest in
preserving the buildings with their original design and materials. Once
a building is a cooperative with many owners, it is hard to get owners
to agree to vacate and demolish, and hence rare for it to be replaced
by a bigger and taller building. In contrast, at the time these buildings
went up, rather often they replaced buildings that had stood for only
30 years or even less.

Daniel Rose characterized Russell Boak as not imposing, unassertive.
Boak was modest enough that there was never a studio portrait of him
in the *Real Estate Forum*, yet assertive enough that, as a very young man,
he left the very active Emery Roth practice to set up a new firm. He was
late to apply for membership in the American Institute of Architects or
even to get his own license as an architect, but quick to adopt innovative
features such as corner casement windows and dropped living rooms
when they were new. Their buildings presented challenges such as
plots with irregular shape, underground streams, and changing building
technologies.

When I first started this project, I made many trips to the Municipal
Archives to look at microfilm of Buildings Department records from
1927 onward. I could only watch the microfilm for about two hours,
so I would leave and go out to look for the building I had turned up.
As I came closer, I would ask myself, would the Boak & Paris building
still be standing at the address, and would I know it when I saw it? The
answer was Yes, and then Yes -- usually I knew it immediately as I turned
the corner into the block.

---

261   *The New York Times*, July 5, 2009.

Today, the Boak & Paris and Boak & Raad apartment buildings have a variety of ownerships and managements. A good number are cooperatives and a few are condominiums, while a relative few are still rental buildings. While some are protected by being within the boundaries of historic districts, all of them appear to be fully occupied and in good to excellent repair. It is hoped that knowing more about the architects and their portfolio of buildings will help these owners, boards, managers, residents and the general public appreciate the treasures with which they are entrusted.

APPENDICES

List of Buildings

*   Located within historic districts designated by the New York City Landmarks Preservation Commission

**   Individual landmarks designated by the Landmarks Preservation Commission

All are apartment buildings in Manhattan unless otherwise noted. Only major commercial buildings included. Numerous minor alterations omitted.

Boak & Paris (1927-42)

1927-28   Broad Park Lodge, 242 Main Street and 2 Westchester Avenue, White Plains, New York; for Pariboke Realty

1927-28   225 West 106th Street, NEC Broadway; for William J. Hanna and Albert P. Frymier

1927-28   *139 East 94th Street, NWC Lexington Avenue; for Samuel Levy

1928-29   9 Prospect Park West, SWC President Street, Brooklyn; for Samuel Wander

1929-31   *302 West 12th Street, SEC Eighth Avenue; for Bing & Bing

1929-30   127 West 96th Street, Amsterdam-Columbus Avenues; for Ralph Ciluzzi

1929-30   Park Vista, 444 Central Park West, NWC 104th Street; for William J. Hanna

1930-31   227 East 57th Street, Second-Third Avenues; for William M. Baumgarten

1930-31   *450 West End Avenue, SEC 82nd Street; for Jacob M. Simon

1930-31   *45 Christopher Street, Waverly Place; for Bing & Bing

1930-31   *315 Riverside Drive, SEC 104th Street; for Arlington C. Hall

1930-31   *22 Riverside Drive, NEC 74th Street; for Arlington C. Hall

1931-32   2375 Marion Avenue, NWC 184th Street, Bronx; for Samuel Aginsky

1931-32   Gun Hill Road, NWC Putnam Place, Bronx; for Sam Minskoff

1931-32   245 Gun Hill Road, King's College Place-Putnam Place, Bronx; for Sam Minskoff

1931-32   *336 West End Avenue, SEC 76th Street; for Frank Sox

1932-33   **Midtown (now Metro) Theater, 2626 Broadway, 99th-100th Streets; for Arlington C. Hall

1933-34   **3320-38 Broadway, 134th-135th Streets, remodeling of Claremont Theater designed by Gaetano Ajello, 1914, to automobile showroom; for Arlington C. Hall

1933-34   *3 East 66th Street, Fifth-Madison Avenues; for Sam Minskoff

1934-35   405 East 72nd Street, First-York Avenues; for Sam Minskoff

1935   *143 West 72nd Street, Amsterdam-Columbus Avenues; alterations to commercial building; for Arlington C. Hall

1936   77 Cooper Street, SEC 207th Street; for Leo Allen Minskoff

1936   *50 East 78th Street, Madison-Park Avenues; for Sam Minskoff

1936   250 Cabrini Boulevard, SWC 187th Street; for Sam Minskoff

1936-37   99 Marble Hill Avenue, SWC 228th Street; for Sidney J. Bernstein

1936-37   *5 Riverside Drive, SEC 73rd Street; for Aaron Simon

1936-37   255 Cabrini Boulevard, NEC 187th Street; for Sam Minskoff

1937-38   *5 West 86th Street, Central Park West-Columbus Avenues; for Irving Broff

1937   110 East 87th Street, Park-Lexington Avenues; for Sydney J. Bernstein

1937   152 East 94th Street, Lexington-Third Avenues; for Sam Minskoff

1937-38   *100 Riverside Drive, SEC 82nd Street; for Aaron Simon

1937-38   508 West 166th Street, Audubon-Amsterdam Avenues; for M. J. Hanover

1937-38   160 East 89th Street, Lexington-Third Avenues; for Arthur Diamond

1937-38   804 Lexington Avenue, NWC 62nd Street; two-story commercial building for Arthur F. Davis

1937   The Dorset, 150 West 79th Street, Amsterdam-Columbus Avenues; major remodeling of building designed by Schwartz & Gross, 1910

1938-39   *The Leonori, 701 Madison Ave. 26 East 63rd St.; major remodeling of building designed by Buchman & Fox, 1901

1939   1200 Grant Avenue, SEC East 167th Street, Bronx; one-story commercial; for Sam Minskoff.

1939   231 Sherman Avenue, NEC 207th Street; for David Zipkin

1939   Mamaronack & Martine Avenues, White Plains, New York, one-story commercial; for Sam Minskoff

1939   251 Seaman Avenue, 215th-218th Streets; for David Zipkin

1939-40   170 East 77th Street, Lexington-Third Avenues; for Arthur Diamond

1939-40   *20 Fifth Avenue, SWC 9th Street; for Aaron Simon

1939-41   37 East 50th Street, Madison-Park Avenues; two-story restaurant for Arlington C. Hall. First rented to Howard Johnson; now Maloney & Porcelli

1940   The Westmore, 333 West 57th Street and 340 West 58th Street, Eighth-Ninth Avenues; for David Rose

1940-41   177 East 77th Street, Lexington-Third Avenues; for Arthur and Sidney Diamond

Boak & Raad (1944-1965)

1945-46   The Thornley, 215 East 79th Street, Second-Third Avenues; for David Rose

1945-48   36 Sutton Place South, NWC 55th Street; for William E. P. Doelger

1947-49   Halsey House, 63-33 98th Place, 63rd Road-63rd Drive, Rego Park, Queens; for Sam Minskoff & Sons

1949-50   440 East 56th Street, First Avenue-Sutton Place South; for William E. P. Doelger

1949-51   Park Gramercy House, 7 Lexington Avenue, SEC 22nd Street; for David Rose & Associates

1950-52   430 East 56th Street, First Avenue-Sutton Place South; for William E. P. Doelger

1952-53   15 North Broadway, Main Sreet and Hamilton Avenue, White Plains; for Improved Risk Mutuals owner, Sam Minskoff & Sons, builders

1952-54   55 Church Street, White Plains; four-story office building for Sam Minskoff & Sons

1952-55   20 Sutton Place South, SWC 56th Street; for William E. P. Doelger

1954-55   412 East 55th Street, First Avenue-Sutton Place South; for William E. P. Doelger

1954-55   *Randall House, 63 East Ninth Street, WS Broadway to Tenth Street; for David Rose & Associates

1954-56   *The Brevoort, 11 Fifth Avenue, Eighth to Ninth Streets; for Sam Minskoff & Sons

1954-56   *20 East 68th Street, SWC Madison Avenue; for David Rose & Associates

1954-56   The Eastmore, 240 East 76th Street, SWC Second Avenue; for David Rose & Associates. Leo Stillman, AIA, Boak & Raad, associate architects

1955-56   220 West Rittenhouse Square, Philadelphia, PA; for E. J. Frankel

1956-59   165 East 72nd & 186 East 73rd Streets, Third Avenue; for J. J. Secoles

1957-58   Westminster House, 55 East 85th Street, NEC Madison Avenue and 52 East 86th Street, Madison-Park Avenues; for Stanley Broff

1957-58   Forest Hills Branch of Queens Borough Public Library, 108-19 71st Avenue, Forest Hills

1958-60   The Hawthorne, 211 East 53rd Street, Second-Third Avenues; for Rose Associates

1958-61   136 East 76th Street, NEC Lexington Avenue; for Irving Seidman & Chester Soling

1958-60   130 East 63rd Street, SWC Lexington Avenue; for Simon Brothers

1958-61   Embassy House, 301 East 47th Street, ES Second Avenue to 48th Street; for Geller & Mitchell

1959-60   The Gaylord, 251 East 51st Street, NWC Second Avenue; for Irving Seidman & Chester Soling

1960-63   8 East 83rd Street, Fifth-Madison Avenues; for Joseph P. Blitz

1960-63   Hemisphere House, 60 West 57th Street and 65 West 56th Street, ES Sixth Avenue; for Andros Realty Corporation

1963   *2 Horatio Street, SWC Greenwich Avenue, western addition to original 1929-31 building by Robert T. Lyons; for Bing & Bing

1961-64   Leland House, 945-955 and 910-920 Underhill Avenue, on Bruckner Boulevard, Bronx; Mitchell-Lama program for Rose Associates

1962-64   29 Broadway, NWC Morris Street, addition to office building 1929-31 Sloan & Robertson; for Andros Realty Corporation

1964   Murray Park, 120 East 34th Street, Park-Lexington Avenues; for Cooper-Bregstein Realty Company

Russell M. Boak Associates (1965-73)

1961-65   *Brevoort East, 20 East Ninth Street to Eighth Street on University Place; for Sam Minskoff & Sons

1965-66   The Homestead, 80 East Hartsdale Avenue, Hartsdale, New York; for Rose Associates

1965-67   Tower 53, 825 Seventh Avenue & 159 West 53rd Street; for Loew's Theatres & Hotels; owner's consultant, Rose Associates

ILLUSTRATION CREDITS

Photographs by author: Pages 28, 29, 107

Photograph by Barbara Probst Morrow: Back cover

Photograph by Peter Mauss, courtesy of Friends of Terra Cotta: Front cover

Photographs by Susan Tunick: Pages 42, 52

Photograph on Frontispiece: Wikimedia, Beyond My Ken

Courtesy of the New York Real Estate Brochure Collection, Avery Architectural and Fine Arts Library, Columbia University: Pages 46, 74, 123, 126, 140, 148, 152, 154

Courtesy of Minskoff Grant Realty and Management Corporation: Pages 136, 155, 167

Collection of Museum of the City of New York/Art Resource, NY: Pages 62, 65, 67, 77, 84, 89, 128, 130, 150, 169

Collection of The New-York Historical Society: Pages 41, 49, 106

Courtesy of New York Public Library, Milstein Division of United States History, Local History & Genealogy, The New York Public Library, Astor, Lenox and Tilden Foundations: Page 70; Art & Architecture Collection, Miriam and Ira D. Wallach Division of Art, Prints and Photographs, The New York Public Library, Astor, Lenox and Tilden Foundations, courtesy of Hanley Wood: Page 86

Courtesy of Office of Metropolitan History: Pages 80, 82, 88, 91

Courtesy of Real Estate Forum/ALM Media, LLC: Page 172

Courtesy of Rose Associates: Pages 102, 103, 109, 118, 134, 144, 158

INDEX

A

B

C

T

V

W

Z

Made in the USA
Lexington, KY
13 November 2014